Dr. Math® Presents More
GEOMETRY

Dr. Math® Presents More GEOMETRY

· · · · · · · · · ·

Learning Geometry Is Easy! Just Ask Dr. Math!

THE MATH FORUM
DREXEL UNIVERSITY

Cartoons by Jessica Wolk-Stanley

WILEY

JOHN WILEY & SONS, INC.

Published by John Wiley & Sons, Inc., Hoboken, New Jersey
Published simultaneously in Canada

Design and composition by Navta Associates, Inc.

For general information about our other products and services, please contact our Customer Care Department within the United States at (800) 762-2974, outside the United States at (317) 572-3993 or fax (317) 572-4002.

Wiley also publishes its books in a variety of electronic formats. Some content that appears in print may not be available in electronic books. For more information about Wiley products, visit our web site at www.wiley.com.

Library of Congress Cataloging-in-Publication Data:

Dr. Math presents more geometry : learning geometry is easy! just ask Dr. Math! / the Math Forum @ Drexel.
    p. cm.
  Includes index.
  ISBN 0-471-22553-3 (pbk.)
1. Geometry—Study and teaching—Juvenile literature. 2. Geometry—Miscellanea—Juvenile literature. I. Title: Doctor Math presents more geometry. II. Math Forum @ Drexel.
  QA445.5.D75 2005
  516—dc22   2004014943

Printed in the United States of America

10 9 8 7 6 5 4 3 2 1

This book is dedicated to
Sarah Seastone (1937–2003),
who loved to play with geometry,
and who gave countless hours to Ask Dr. Math
as editor, archivist, and Math Doctor.

Contents..

Acknowledgments..........................

Suzanne Alejandre and Melissa Running created this book based on the work of the Math Doctors, with lots of help from Math Forum employees, past and present:

> Annie Fetter, Problem of the Week administrator and geometry consultant
>
> Ian Underwood, Attending Physician
>
> Sarah Seastone, Editor and Archivist
>
> Tom Epp, Archivist
>
> Lynne Steuerle and Frank Wattenberg, Contributors to the original plans
>
> Kristina Lasher, Associate Director of Programs
>
> Stephen Weimar, Director of the Math Forum

We are indebted to Jerry Lyons for his valuable advice and encouragement. Our editors at Wiley, Kate Bradford and Kimberly Monroe-Hill, have been of great assistance.

Our heartfelt thanks goes out to the hundreds of Math Doctors who've given so generously of their time and talents over the years, and without whom no one could Ask Dr. Math. We'd especially like to thank those Math Doctors whose work is the basis of this book:

Anthony Hugh Back, Pat Ballew, Michael Barrus, Guy Brandenburg, D. J. Brasier, Michael F. Collins, Bob Davies, Tom Davis, Patrick Donahue, Chita Duval, Annie Fetter, Tim Greene, Byron Holz, Mark Jaffee, Floor van Lamoen, Ethan Magness, Maryanthe Malliaris, Jerry Mathews, Josh Mitteldorf, Paul Narula, Dave Peterson, Rick Peterson, Melissa Running, Sarah Seastone, Robert Shimmin, Santu de Silva, Rachel Sullivan, Ian Underwood, Peter Wang, Robert L.

Ward, Steve Weimar, John Wilkinson, Ken Williams, and Joshua Zucker.

Drexel University graciously hosts and supports The Math Forum, reflecting its role as a leader in the application of technology to undergraduate and graduate education.

Introduction ....

You will have learned a lot of geometry before you take an official course called "geometry," which most people take in high school. Much of this previous study involves learning about different figures and their properties and calculating things like lengths, angles, areas, and perimeters.

You'll do more of this in a geometry course, which is what this book is about. Some of it will be a review, while some of it will incorporate new facts and ideas. But you'll also begin to learn to explain *why* you know your answers are correct and *how* you know that certain statements you make are true.

You may have learned some theorems before, but now, for many of them, you'll also learn how to explain why they have to be true. And if you think about a theorem and figure it out on your own (which is what people mean when they say that they "prove" a theorem), then you have really learned a lot.

If you have access to geometry software, you might try using it to investigate some of the theorems that you're learning. A theorem is a lot easier to prove if you actually believe that it's true! You can also use the software to try to figure out answers to problems you're asked to solve. Once you've found the answer, the software might help you figure out why that *must* be the correct conclusion.

Don't get too worried about writing proofs and explanations. Think of them as puzzles that you can solve.

Here are a few other tips that will help you succeed in geometry:

Geometry can seem almost like learning a foreign language. There are a lot of vocabulary words and formulas to remember, as well as names of figures and their properties.

Think about *what the words and their parts mean*! That can help a lot (and not just in geometry, or even math). Use a dictionary to look up words you don't understand.

Concentrate on *understanding concepts*, not memorizing a zillion little facts that you can look up later. For example, if you understand the concept of area and some pretty basic ideas of how you can calculate it, you don't really need to know the area formula for *every* figure you learn about. You can always figure it out when you need it. (You may notice that most of the standardized tests you take, such as the SATs, provide you with a formulas sheet. This emphasizes the fact that memorizing the formulas isn't as important as understanding and knowing how to use them.)

Don't try to memorize all of the properties of every individual figure you learn about. Instead, try to concentrate on *how the different groups of figures are related*. Many of the properties of one figure will apply to others related to it, and you'll have a better understanding of that "family" of objects.

As with any math course, *read over the next section in the book before class*. You don't have to try to understand it, but at least the words and ideas will seem familiar to you when they're talked about in class.

Draw lots of pictures, even if the problem seems short and simple. And write down all of your steps, no matter how trivial they may seem. It's really easy to make small mistakes that will throw off the rest of your work. Along the same lines, don't erase work that you've done. You might want to write it off to one side, but keep it so that you have a record of what you did. Don't try to write out a final version of a proof before you do some scribbling and write some rough drafts (and don't throw out those rough drafts!).

Finally, figure out *what resources work well for you* when you need help or if you want to learn more. If your teacher is available outside of class and explains things well, great. But you might find that you do better consulting your textbook or a book like this to see things explained another way. There are also many Web sites about every possible geometry topic. Some of those sites are listed at the ends of the sections of these books.

And, of course, the Dr. Math Web site has a lot of questions and answers about geometry that don't appear in this book. If you don't find the answer there, don't forget that you can always Ask Dr. Math yourself!

PART 1

Points, Lines, Planes, Angles, and Their Relationships

Points, lines, and planes are the building blocks of geometry. Everything else we do depends on an understanding of what these three words mean. However, these three words are undefined! There is no way to write a definition of them based on other terms in geometry. But we can agree on general descriptions of these objects.

It seems weird to think that the geometry we're used to is built on a few terms we can't define. But I guess you've got to start somewhere.

Yeah. It sounds like the kind of geometry you get depends on what you assume at the beginning. Kind of like cooking—what you make depends on the ingredients you put in.

- A *point* is simply a location. It doesn't have length or width or any size at all.
- A *line* is a collection of points that has infinite length and is straight, but that doesn't have any width.
- A *plane* is a flat surface that extends forever in all directions.

Once we have an idea of what these three objects look like, we can use them to define a lot of other objects in geometry, such as *segments*, *rays*, and *angles*, and can develop concepts such as *parallel*, *perpendicular*, and *congruent*.

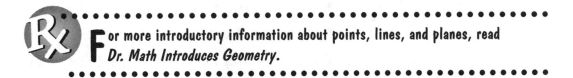

For more introductory information about points, lines, and planes, read *Dr. Math Introduces Geometry*.

Just as we have undefined terms in geometry, we also have some other building blocks called **postulates**. These are statements that we agree to accept as true even though we can't prove them, and then we derive the rest of geometry from them. The mathematician Euclid wrote a book called *The Elements* in which he started out with five postulates and developed a system of geometry from them.

Much of what you will learn in geometry is called *Euclidean geometry*. This type of geometry assumes that Euclid's parallel postulate is true—that is, given a line and a point not on the line, there is exactly one line through the given point that is parallel to the given line.

Since this is a postulate, that means we can't prove it's true. In the study of Euclidean geometry, we assume it is true. But there are other kinds of geometry (which you can read about at the end of this part) that assume Euclid's parallel postulate isn't true.

In this part, Dr. Math explains

- angle relationships and perpendicular and parallel lines
- proving lines parallel
- the parallel postulate
- coordinates and distance

Angle Relationships and Perpendicular and Parallel Lines

An important part of geometry involves finding angle measures and showing how different angles are related. Perpendicular lines meet at a right angle. Parallel lines are coplanar lines (lines on the same plane) that never intersect. In this part, we'll talk about different relationships between angles in a figure, including special angle relationships that are formed when parallel lines are crossed by a transversal.

Adjacent Angles

Dear Dr. Math,

I would appreciate it if you could answer my question: How do you define adjacent angles? We're learning about linear pairs in my class, and I think it has something to do with those.

Yours truly,

Qian (pronounced "Chen")

Hi, Qian,

Adjacent angles share a vertex and a common side between them but have no interior points in common. In the diagram shown below, ∠ADB and ∠BDC are adjacent angles.

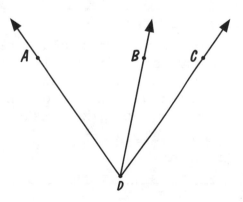

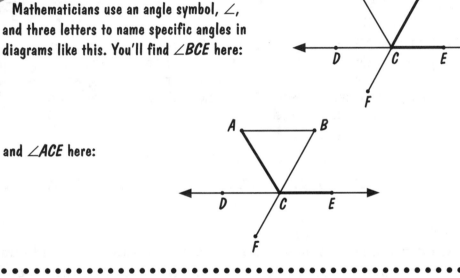

If you're learning about **linear pairs of angles,** you probably know that they are a pair of angles whose outer edges lie on one line. Do you see how this leads you to adjacent angles?

—*Dr. Math, The Math Forum*

NAMING ANGLES

Mathematicians use an angle symbol, $\angle$, and three letters to name specific angles in diagrams like this. You'll find $\angle BCE$ here:

and $\angle ACE$ here:

Angles in a Diagram	Dear Dr. Math, I've got perpendicular, parallel, and transversal lines all connected and labeled with letters. Some of the angle measures are marked. I have to find the rest of them. How do I do this? Yours truly, Quentin

Hi, Quentin,

Isn't that nice of them to give you some of the degrees? Actually, it isn't as bad as it sounds. I'll give you an example. I bet you'll find most of this familiar from math class.

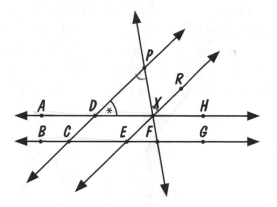

Suppose $\overleftrightarrow{CP}$ and $\overleftrightarrow{ER}$ are parallel, and $\overleftrightarrow{AH}$ and $\overleftrightarrow{BG}$ are parallel, too, and $\overleftrightarrow{CP}$, $\overleftrightarrow{ER}$, and $\overleftrightarrow{FP}$ are transversals to $\overleftrightarrow{AH}$ and $\overleftrightarrow{BG}$. Suppose they gave you the measure of the angle I have marked with a *, namely $\angle PDX$.

We know that **vertical angles** are equal (or **congruent**, as they say). What is the vertical angle that goes with $\angle PDX$? When two lines cross each other to form sort of the letter x, the opposite angles of the letter x are equal; in this case, $\angle PDX$ and $\angle ADC$.

We know that **corresponding angles** are congruent. Corresponding angles are found when parallel lines are crossed with a transversal. Is $\angle PDX$ one of a pair of corresponding angles? Yes: $\angle PDX$ and $\angle DCE$. The two angles are in corresponding positions relative to the intersection of the transversal with each of the parallel lines $\overleftrightarrow{AH}$ and $\overleftrightarrow{BG}$.

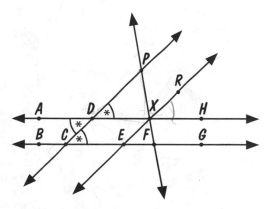

We know that **alternate interior angles** are congruent and that **alternate exterior angles** are congruent, too. Alternate interior angles are also found when parallel lines are crossed with a transversal. Is $\angle PDX$ one of a pair of alternate interior angles? Yes: $\angle PDX$ and $\angle DXE$. Both of these angles are on the interior of the two parallel lines $\overleftrightarrow{CP}$ and $\overleftrightarrow{ER}$, and they are on alternate sides of the transversal $\overleftrightarrow{AH}$. Is $\angle PDX$ one of a pair of alternate exterior angles? Yes, though we'd need to put another point on the unlabeled extension of ray $\overleftrightarrow{DC}$ in order to name the other angle.

Now, if $\overleftrightarrow{ER}$ and $\overleftrightarrow{CP}$ are parallel, then $\angle PDX$ and $\angle RXH$ are corresponding angles, too. So they're congruent:

Now that we know $\angle RXH$, we can find its vertical angles, its corresponding angles, and so on. Each time you find an angle, check if it has angles congruent to it (vertical, corresponding, alternating, and so on); then for each of those, you can find more.

—Dr. Math, The Math Forum

Isn't it great to be able to "see" geometry?

Yes, the way they solve the problems sounds so stuffy, but when I look at the diagrams, it helps me understand what they're trying to say.

Geometry Proofs: Lines and Planes

Dear Dr. Math,

Can you help me prove the following three theorems?

Theorem 1-1: If two lines intersect, then they intersect at exactly one point.

Theorem 1-2: Through a line and a point not on the line there is exactly one plane.

Theorem 1-3: If two lines intersect, then exactly one plane contains the lines.

Sincerely,

Qian

Hi, Qian,

I don't know just what postulates and theorems you have to start with. Each math book does things a little differently. But since you've been given these to prove yourself, you can guess that they can't be too hard, so everything you need is probably right there in the chapter. I'll give you the basic ideas, and you can fill in the details based on what you know.

Theorem 1-1: You know that the lines intersect (at a minimum of one point), so you need to prove that they can't intersect at two (or more) points. Suppose they did intersect at two points, *A* and *B*. You probably have a postulate or a theorem that there is only one line between any two points. Do you see how this tells you that what we've supposed is impossible?

Theorem 1-2: You probably have a theorem or a postulate that there is only one plane through three points that are not **collinear** (on the same line). Given a line and a point not on the line, you can pick any two points on the line and you'll have three points to use. Now you have to prove that not only those three points but the whole line is in the plane. You may have a theorem that already says that.

Theorem 1-3: Again, if two lines intersect, you can pick three points to define a plane. You have to prove that both lines are in the plane.

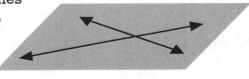

You can use what you proved in theorem 1-2 to show that both lines are in this plane.

—*Dr. Math, The Math Forum*

DO PARALLEL LINES INTERSECT?

Parallel lines do not intersect. In fact, that is the definition of parallel lines in a plane. Perspective drawing might be confusing this idea. In perspective drawing, parallel lines appear to intersect eventually (imagine straight railroad tracks that are going off into the distance). In art, the point where the lines appear to intersect is called the vanishing point. In geometry, it's called the point at infinity.

Slopes of Perpendicular Lines

Dear Dr. Math,

Our class has been working on graphing lines. I know that the product of the opposite reciprocals of the slopes of perpendicular lines that are not vertical and horizontal is −1. I see how it works, but I don't understand how you get this number. Could you show me the proof that justifies this answer? Thanks a lot.

Yours truly,
Quentin

Hi, Quentin,

You've combined two different ways of saying the same thing, but I understand what you mean. You can say either that the slopes of perpendicular lines are "opposite reciprocals" of each other (that is, $m_2 = \frac{-1}{m_1}$) or that the product of their slopes is –1 (that is, $m_1 \cdot m_2 = -1$). These equations say the same thing.

Let's draw a quick picture and see what this means:

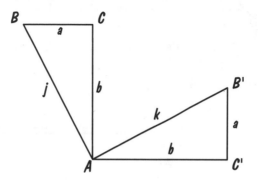

Lines j and k are perpendicular. I've drawn a right triangle ABC with its **legs** (the short sides of a right triangle) parallel to the axes and its **hypotenuse** (the longest side of a right triangle, opposite the right angle) along j, then rotated it 90 degrees so that the hypotenuse of $AB'C'$ is along k. Since each leg has been rotated 90 degrees, AC' and $B'C'$ are now parallel to the axes, but they have switched axes. So the slope of j is $\frac{-b}{a}$ (negative because when we go right a distance of a, we go down a distance of b), and the slope of k is $\frac{a}{b}$. So the product of the slopes is

$$m_1 \cdot m_2 = -\frac{b}{a} \cdot \frac{a}{b} = -1$$

There's your proof. Whenever I think of the slopes of perpendicular lines, I think of this diagram.

—Dr. Math, The Math Forum

Ⓡ𝕏 **D**on't forget, if you need more help with lines and slope, check out our book *Dr. Math Explains Algebra.*

Proving Lines Parallel

Earlier we looked at ways of finding the measures of various angles that were formed by parallel lines cut by a transversal. We can now use those same techniques in reverse to show that two (or more) lines are parallel.

Parallel Lines

Dear Dr. Math,

What are some ways of proving lines parallel?

Sincerely,

Qian

Hi, Qian,

There are lots of ways to prove lines parallel. It depends on what you are given to work with. Are you using coordinates and equations in algebra or drawing lines and looking for congruent angles in geometry?

I'll get you started by listing a couple of ways to prove lines parallel.

1. *Slope:* If both lines have the same slope, they are parallel. So if you know the equations for both lines and you can see that both equations have the same slope, you know the lines are parallel. Do you remember that slope is m in equations of the form $y = mx + b$? So, for example, in the two equations $y = -3x + 7$ and $y = -3x + 4$, the slopes are both -3, which means the lines are parallel.

2. *Pairs of angles:* Suppose we have three lines all in the same plane, j, k, and l. Say that line k makes a 30-degree angle with line j and a 30-degree angle with line l as in the diagram on the following page. Those two angles are corresponding angles, and if corresponding angles are equal, then the two lines are

parallel. So *j* and *l* must be parallel. There will also be situations where you might find equal alternate interior angles or equal alternate exterior angles.

How many other ways can you think of to prove lines parallel?

—*Dr. Math, The Math Forum*

Here's another one! If the same side interior angles formed by a single line crossing two other lines add up to 180 degrees, then the two lines being crossed are parallel.

Hey, isn't that one way of stating Euclid's fifth postulate?

The Parallel Postulate

One of the most fascinating aspects of mathematics is that there are statements that no one has proven to be true or false! Perhaps the most famous of these is Euclid's controversial fifth postulate, which is paraphrased as for every line *l* and point *P* not on that line, there exists a unique line *m* through *P* that is parallel to *l*.

Throughout history, almost from the postulate's conception, mathematicians have tried in vain to prove or disprove it. It seems that Euclid himself did not entirely trust the postulate, for he avoided using it as long as he could in his great work, *The Elements*, by proving his first twenty-eight propositions without it. While the geometry you typically study in school assumes that the postulate is true, it's good to understand that there are other kinds of geometries.

The Role of Postulates

Dear Dr. Math,

I'm in Euclidean geometry, and the teacher said that theorems are proven; postulates are not. Why? Who decided what were postulates and what were theorems? I asked my teacher if postulates could be proven and simply weren't, and she said that they couldn't be proven.

Postulates come first, then theorems are formed from those postulates (right?). So the entire geometry is based on postulates that weren't and can't be proven. That just doesn't seem right to me. Could you explain why it's okay that they're not proven?

Yours truly,

Quentin

Hi, Quentin,

The basic answer to your question is that we have to start somewhere. The essence of mathematics (introduced by the Greeks) is to take a small set of fundamental facts called postulates or axioms and build from them a full understanding of the objects you are dealing with (whether numbers, shapes, or something else entirely) using only logical reasoning such that if people accept the postulates, then they must agree with you on the rest.

These postulates may be (and were for the Greeks) basic assumptions or observations about the way things really are, or they may just be suppositions you make for the sake of imagining something with no necessary connection with the real world. In the first case, we want to choose facts as postulates that are so obvious that no one would question them; in the second case, we are free to assume whatever we want. In both cases, we want a minimal set of postulates so that we are assuming as little as possible and can't prove one from another.

Euclid's problem was that one of the postulates (the fifth) didn't seem simple enough, so over the centuries people tried to prove it from the other postulates rather than be forced to accept something that didn't seem immediately obvious. Eventually it was realized that there are in fact different kinds of geometry, some of which don't follow all of Euclid's postulates; and that you could replace his parallel postulate with a contradictory assumption and still have a workable system. In particular, spherical geometry—the way things work on a sphere, where a "line" is a circle whose center is the center of the sphere—is an example of this, in which parallel lines just don't exist. Spherical geometry follows different rules yet is just as valid as plane geometry.

So we have to take as our starting point some postulates that simply define the particular mathematical system we are studying. If we take a different set of postulates, we get a different system, which may be just as useful as the original—and therefore just as true—yet different in its conclusions. The postulates we choose are the connection between the abstract concepts about which we are making proofs and the real-world ideas that they model (if any). Without postulates, we would not have such a connection and would be reasoning about nothing!

—Dr. Math, The Math Forum

Dear Dr. Math,

Is it possible to draw a triangle with more than 180 degrees?

Yours truly,

Qian

Hi, Qian,

If we suppose that we're drawing triangles on a flat sheet of paper, it's impossible to draw a triangle with more than 180 degrees. I've drawn a diagram for you that may help:

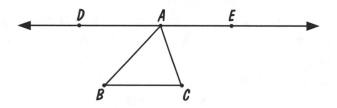

Suppose that we have a triangle with vertices A, B, and C. You've probably learned that we can draw a single line DE through A parallel to BC; that's how it works in Euclidean geometry. Now suppose we consider $\angle EAC$. We know that it's the same measure as $\angle ACB$, which is in the triangle, because they are alternate interior angles. Also, for the same reason we know that $\angle DAB$ is the same measure as $\angle ABC$.

So we see that $m\angle DAB + m\angle BAC + m\angle EAC = m\angle ABC + m\angle BAC + m\angle ACB$ (where m means measure). But the first half of that equation equals 180 degrees, since three angles on the same side of a line fill that half of the line (that is, they add up to a "straight angle" of 180 degrees). Thus, the angles in the triangle also add up to 180 degrees: on a flat sheet of paper, a triangle has exactly 180 degrees.

However, in a different geometry, a triangle might have more degrees. Consider a "triangle" on a globe that includes the north pole and two points on the equator. Here the two angles on the equator will be 90 degrees, plus there'll be the angle at the north pole, which could be as much as 180 degrees. In this case, the triangle must have more degrees than 180.

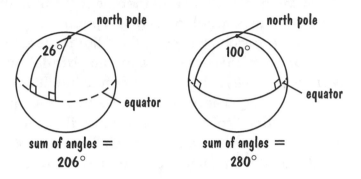

sum of angles = 206°   sum of angles = 280°

The difference is that the rule about parallel lines doesn't work on the sphere, whereas it does on the flat plane.

This is just the very beginning of non-Euclidean geometry; it gets much harder.

—*Dr. Math, The Math Forum*

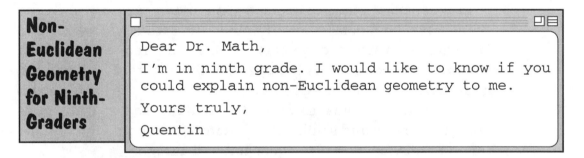

Non-Euclidean Geometry for Ninth-Graders

Dear Dr. Math,

I'm in ninth grade. I would like to know if you could explain non-Euclidean geometry to me.

Yours truly,

Quentin

Hi, Quentin,

Euclidean geometry assumes that the Euclidean parallel postulate is true. The postulate states that given any line and any point not on that line, there is exactly one line through that point that is parallel to the given line. It is important to remember that "parallel" always means "lines that never intersect"—that is, "lines that share no common point," *not* "lines that are the same distance apart everywhere." Parallel lines in non-Euclidean geometries may be closer to or farther from each other at various points.

Non-Euclidean geometry assumes the "negation" of the Euclidean parallel postulate: there is some line and some point on that line such that either (A) there is no line through that point that is parallel to the given line, or (B) there is more than one line through that point that is parallel to the given point.

As it turns out, you can show that if case A happens somewhere in your geometry, then there are no parallel lines *anywhere in your whole geometry*. This is pretty amazing. It means that every pair of lines in this geometry will intersect somewhere. This kind of geometry is called "spherical" or "elliptical" geometry. You can model it on the surface of a sphere, which I'll talk about later.

As a consequence, you can show that if case B happens anywhere in your geometry, then it happens *everywhere*, too. We call this geometry "hyperbolic" geometry. In this geometry, given any line and any point not on that line, there is more than one line through that point that is parallel to the given line. As it turns out, you can then show that there are *infinitely many* such parallel lines through your given point and your given line.

In these other kinds of geometry, it's often necessary to define "point" and "line" somewhat differently from what we are used to. For example, in spherical geometry, a line is a "great circle," which is a circle whose center is the center of the sphere. Think about a great circle or a "line" that goes through the north pole and the south pole of Earth. Now think about rotating that line so that it still goes through the north and south poles, but instead of going through the United States, for example, it goes through Europe.

We know that in any geometry, two points determine a unique line. And it seems like in the example above, we have two lines that go through two points: the north and south poles. So we have to define "point" differently. In spherical geometry, we define a point to be a single point *and* its opposite point. Now the north and south poles are considered a single point. Imagine putting two of these "points" on the sphere, and you'll see that you can only draw one possible line through them. However, you will also notice that every line you draw intersects every other line! So this is a model in which there aren't any parallel lines at all. You can see two great circles in the figure on the following page.

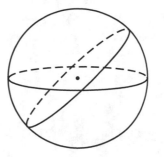

So that's elliptical geometry. Here's a model for hyperbolic geometry. Let the plane you're working in be the upper half of the x-y–plane, without the x-axis—that is, the set of all points where $y > 0$. We call this the open upper half-plane. There are two kinds of lines in this model. One kind will be half-circles whose center is on the x-axis, and the other kind will be lines that are perpendicular to the x-axis. In this model, points are just normal points in the plane.

Draw a couple of "lines" in this model, and note that at best they'll intersect at only one point. Then pick one of the lines you've drawn and take some point not on that line. See how many lines you can draw through that point that are parallel to (don't intersect) the given line. A bunch, right? In the figure below, there are two lines through point A that are "parallel" to line l. So this is hyperbolic geometry.

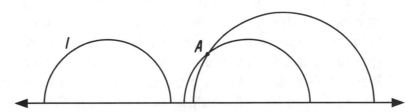

These are just two models of non-Euclidean geometry that mathematicians use. Another one that is often studied in middle and high school is called "taxicab geometry." If you are interested in learning more about it, view the Web resource listed at the end of this section called "Geometry Problem of the Week: Taxicab Distances."

—*Dr. Math, The Math Forum*

Coordinates and Distance

"Coordinate geometry" is based on the coordinate axes and uses the coordinates of points to calculate slopes of lines, midpoints of segments, and distances between points, as well as to define the relationships between lines. You probably learned a lot of coordinate geometry in algebra class, so some of this will look pretty familiar. But there are a few ideas that are especially important in geometry.

When you learn formulas like the ones in this section, don't worry if they seem complicated. They are formulas that you can easily figure out again on your own, as long as you understand how they work. One important thing to remember about the distance formula is that it's just another way of writing the **Pythagorean theorem**. (You remember that, don't you? Where a and b are the legs of a right triangle and c is the hypotenuse, and $a^2 + b^2 = c^2$.) We use it when we have the coordinates of points instead of the lengths of segments. In this section, we'll give examples of ways to use both of these formulas.

Dear Dr. Math,

What is the midpoint of the line segment
whose endpoints are (-3,4) and (5,-2)?

Sincerely,

Qian

Hi, Qian,

To find the midpoint of that segment, we could use the midpoint formula, or we could just reason it out. Let's reason it out, then look at
the formula.

Let's draw a right triangle, where the segment we're given is the
hypotenuse. I've drawn it so that the right angle is at the point (5,4).
Now we can find the midpoint of each of the sides of the right triangle. For the top of the triangle, we find the x-coordinate of the midpoint by finding the average of the x-coordinates of the endpoints.
This will be (-3 + 5)/2, which is $\frac{2}{2}$, or 1. So the point is (1,4). We can find
the midpoint of the right-hand side by finding the average of the

y-coordinates of the endpoints.
This gives us (4 + -2)/2, which
is $\frac{2}{2}$, or 1. So that point is (5,1). We
can draw vertical and horizontal
lines through those points, and
they will meet at the midpoint of
the hypotenuse. We have found
the halfway point across and the
halfway point down.

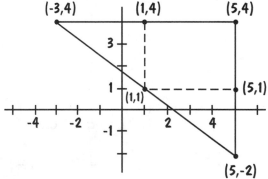

This leads us to the midpoint
formula, which is just a fancy way of writing down all of the work
that we did above. If our two points are (x_1, y_1) and (x_2, y_2), then the
midpoint is

$$\left(\frac{x_1 + x_2}{2} , \frac{y_1 + y_2}{2} \right)$$

—Dr. Math, The Math Forum

Dear Dr. Math,

Can you help me with this problem?

Given a line going through the points (10,10) and (20,15), find the coordinates of a third point on the line that is 3 units from the point (10,10).

Thanks!

Quentin

Hi, Quentin,

To begin with, we need to find the equation of the line. The slope of the line is given by

$$\frac{\text{difference of } y's}{\text{difference of } x's} \text{, which is equal to}$$

$$\frac{(15 - 10)}{(20 - 10)}$$

$$= \frac{5}{10}$$

$$= \frac{1}{2}$$

The equation of the line is

$$y - 10 = \frac{1}{2}(x - 10)$$

$$y - 10 = \frac{1}{2}x - 5$$

$$y = \frac{1}{2}x + 5$$

Let the point that is 3 units from (10,10) be (x,y).

If a point is 3 units from another point, it means that the distance between the two points is 3 units. This in turn means that we can use the distance formula (which comes from the Pythagorean theorem).

The distance formula says that the distance d between two points x_1, y_1 and x_2, y_2 is given by $d^2 = (x_2 - x_1)^2 + (y_2 - y_1)^2$. This makes a little more sense when you look at the following diagram:

The distance between the two points (x_1, y_1) and (x_2, y_2) is the

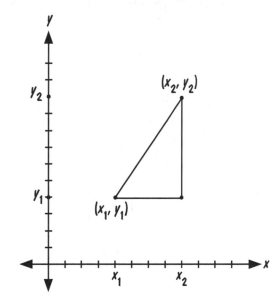

length of the hypotenuse of the above right triangle, correct? We use the Pythagorean theorem to find the length of the hypotenuse of a right triangle. The length of the base of this triangle is $(x_2 - x_1)$. You can also write $(x_1 - x_2)$, because if this happens to be a negative number, it will be squared in the Pythagorean theorem. The height is $(y_2 - y_1)$, which can also be written as $(y_1 - y_2)$. If we call the hypotenuse d, then from the Pythagorean theorem we can write

$$d^2 = (x_2 - x_1)^2 + (y_2 - y_1)^2$$

In our problem, $d = 3$, and we want to find the point (x,y) that is 3 units away from (10,10). So we can write the distance formula as $(x - 10)^2 + (y - 10)^2 = 3^2 = 9$. We substitute $\frac{1}{2}x + 5$ (the equation of our line) for y:

$$(x - 10)^2 + (y - 10)^2 = 9 \qquad \text{Original distance formula}$$

$$(x - 10)^2 + \left(\frac{x}{2} + 5 - 10\right)^2 = 9 \qquad \text{Substituting } y = \frac{1}{2}x + 5$$

$$(x - 10)^2 + \left(\frac{x}{2} - 5\right)^2 = 9 \qquad \text{Simplifying}$$

$$(x - 10)^2 + \left(\frac{x}{2} - \frac{10}{2}\right)^2 = 9 \qquad \text{Finding common denominator}$$

$$(x - 10)^2 + \left(\frac{x - 10}{2}\right)^2 = 9 \qquad \text{Simplifying}$$

$$(x - 10)^2 + \left(\frac{1}{4}\right)(x - 10)^2 = 9 \qquad \text{Factoring out } \left(\frac{1}{2}\right)^2 = \frac{1}{4}$$

$$\left(\frac{5}{4}\right)(x - 10)^2 = 9 \qquad \text{Factoring out } (x - 10)^2$$

$$(x - 10)^2 = \frac{36}{5}$$

$$x - 10 = \frac{\pm 6}{\sqrt{5}}$$

$$x = 10 + \frac{\pm 6}{\sqrt{5}}$$

$$x = 10 + \frac{\pm 6 \cdot \sqrt{5}}{5}$$

We substitute $x = 10 + \dfrac{6 \cdot \sqrt{5}}{5}$ into the equation for our line:

$$y = \frac{1}{2}x + 5 \qquad \text{Equation for line}$$

$$= \left(\frac{1}{2}\right)10 + \frac{6\sqrt{5}}{5} \qquad \text{Substituting}$$

$$= 5 + \frac{3\sqrt{5}}{5} + 5 \qquad\qquad \text{Simplifying}$$

$$= 10 + \frac{3\sqrt{5}}{5}$$

The coordinates of the point that is 3 units from (10,10) are

$$\left(10 + \frac{6\sqrt{5}}{5} ,\ 10 + \frac{3\sqrt{5}}{5} \right)$$

What if we use $x = 10 - \dfrac{6 \cdot \sqrt{5}}{5}$? Then we get another point that is

3 units away from (10,10) but in the opposite direction. Since your problem only asks for one point, we don't need to figure out the coordinates of the other point that is 3 units away from (10,10). Can you figure out why there are only two points on the line that are 3 units away from (10,10)?

—Dr. Math, The Math Forum

esources on the Web

Learn more about points, lines, planes, and angles at these sites:

Math Forum: Geometry Problem of the Week: Points, Lines, and Planes

mathforum.org/geopow/solutions/solution.ehtml?puzzle=202

Determine the number of lines defined by five or six points and the number of planes defined by four or five points. Expand this for *N* points.

Math Forum: Geometry Problem of the Week: Taxicab Distances

mathforum.org/geopow/solutions/solution.ehtml?puzzle=224

Find a general formula for distance in a taxicab geometry universe.

Math Forum: Geometry Problem of the Week: What's My Angle?

mathforum.org/geopow/solutions/solution.ehtml?puzzle=206

Given line AE, point C between A and E, ray CB perpendicular to line AE, and point D on the same side of AE as point B, if CD equals DE and angle CDE is x degrees, what is the angle measure of BCD?

Math Forum: How Far Between Cities? Part I

mathforum.org/te/alejandre/image.cursor/lesson.html

A step-by-step activity encouraging students to see how an applet can be used to form a right triangle on a map.

Math Forum: How Far Between Cities? Part II

mathforum.org/te/alejandre/image.cursor/lesson.a.html

Students learn to apply the Pythagorean theorem to calculate the distance between two points on a map.

Math Forum: Measuring Distances—Triangulation

mathforum.org/paths/measurement/meastriangm.html

Students will determine the distance to an object.

Math Forum: Plane History

mathforum.org/cgraph/history/

Learn about the history of the coordinate plane.

Shodor Organization: Project Interactivate: Angles Activity

shodor.org/interactivate/activities/angles/

This activity allows the user to practice important angle vocabulary. Line l is parallel to line m. Also, line r is parallel to line s. Each of the angles formed by the intersection of these four parallel lines can be classified as acute, obtuse, or right.

Shodor Organization: Project Interactivate: Image Tool Activity

shodor.org/interactivate/activities/imagetool/

Users can measure angles, distances, and areas in several different images (choices include maps, aerial photos, and others). A scale feature allows users to set the scale used for measuring distances and areas.

PART 2

Logic and Proof

The word "geometry" points to its practical origins: it means "measurement of the earth." An ancient Greek named Eratosthenes, among others, used geometry (and its relative, trigonometry, which means "measurement of triangles") to find the circumference of Earth. This was crucial for mapmaking, and many of the same principles apply. Our modern technology relies on many of the same ideas that mathematicians discovered and developed in ancient times.

Geometry is still used in its original sense by surveyors. It's used every second by those Global Positioning System (GPS) devices you may have heard of that can pinpoint where you are using location information from several satellites.

Isn't it interesting to think about how one subject was developed because of another?

Yes. I usually think of each one separately, but I think what Dr. Math says about the connection between logic and geometry makes sense.

But one of the greatest values of geometry traces back to what Euclid did twenty-three hundred years ago. Geometry was revolutionary because it got people thinking logically and reasoning out why something is true. Euclid really set the stage for science, for careful examination of the world, and for the idea of cause and effect. And every year when students study geometry and are introduced to a system of logical thought, it once again sets the stage for some of those students to head into sciences and technical fields that require careful reasoning.

In this part, Dr. Math explains

- introduction to logic
- direct proof
- indirect proof

Introduction to Logic

As we've said, logic is an integral part of all geometry courses. But you've been using logic in your studies of mathematics for a very long time! The basic idea is that you need to be able to explain why each statement you make is true based on other facts that you know (or that you've proved!). This section will give you an introduction to some of the ideas and terminology used in "formal logic," or the study of logic itself.

Determining Truth

Dear Dr. Math,

A number divisible by 2 is divisible by 4. I'm supposed to figure out the hypothesis, the conclusion, and a converse statement; say whether the converse statement is true or false; and if it is false, give a counterexample. I don't understand.

Yours truly,

Qian

Hi, Qian,

You're asking about the terminology of logic, which is important in math to help us talk about proofs and how we know something is true. Words such as "converse" allow us to talk about our reasoning and determine whether we are really making sense.

A statement such as "any number divisible by 2 is divisible by 4" can be rewritten as

If a number N is divisible by 2, then it is divisible by 4

The **hypothesis**, or **premise**, is what is given or supposed, the "if":

N is divisible by 2

The **conclusion** is what is concluded from that, the "then":

N is divisible by 4

The converse of the statement "If a, then b" is "If b, then a," turning the statement around so that the conclusion becomes the hypothesis and the hypothesis becomes the conclusion. In this case, the converse is

If the number N is divisible by 4, then it is divisible by 2

Now we have to consider whether either statement is true. A statement and its converse may be both true, or both false, or one true and the other false; knowing whether one is true says nothing about whether the other is true. In this case, the original statement is false. (This makes me wonder if you copied the problem wrong; it doesn't sound like this possibility was considered in the question.) How do I know it's false? Because I can give a counterexample: a number N for which the hypothesis is true but the conclusion is false. Can you see what I can use for N that is even but not divisible by 4?

However, the converse is true. Can you see why? You might just try listing lots of numbers that are divisible by 4. Are they all even? If all your examples are even, you haven't proven anything, but the list may suggest to you a reason why you will never be able to find a counterexample. That reason would be the basis of a proof.

—*Dr. Math, The Math Forum*

Dear Dr. Math,

The directions say, "Write the converse, inverse, and contrapositive of each conditional. Determine if the converse, inverse, and contapostive are true or false. If false, give a counterexample." I can't seem to do these:

All squares are quadrilaterals.

If a ray bisects an angle, then the two angles formed are congruent.

Vertical angles are congruent.

Yours truly,

Quentin

Hi, Quentin,

Let's make sure you're clear on the meanings of **converse**, **inverse**, and **contrapositive**. These words are used in the context of a **conditional statement**—that is, a logic sentence with a condition in it. This includes sentences of the form

"if p, then q"

The converse of any such sentence is

"if q, then p"

We've flipped the hypothesis and conclusion in the sentence. The inverse is

"if not p, then not q"

We've negated both halves of the sentence. And the contrapositive is

"if not q, then not p"

This is the combination of the converse and the inverse in a way: we've flipped the hypothesis and conclusion, *and* we've negated both halves of the resulting sentence.

The problem with two of your statements is that they don't neatly fit into the "if p, then q" format, so you need to first find *equivalent* sentences of the form "if p, then q."

Your first example says that "all squares are quadrilaterals." That is the same as saying, "If x is a square, then x is a quadrilateral."

Your second example is already in the right form, since it consists of an "if" statement and a "then" statement.

And your third example is just like your first example. See if you can finish it.

—*Dr. Math, The Math Forum*

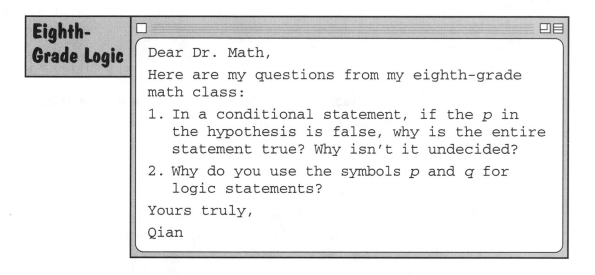

Dear Dr. Math,

Here are my questions from my eighth-grade math class:

1. In a conditional statement, if the *p* in the hypothesis is false, why is the entire statement true? Why isn't it undecided?

2. Why do you use the symbols *p* and *q* for logic statements?

Yours truly,

Qian

Hi, Qian,

Let me answer your second question first. The use of p and q in logic statements began around 1900, but it's not clear why these letters were chosen. We might guess that it was because the beginning and end of the alphabet were already heavily used in algebra, but no one really knows.

Now for the hard question: if the p in the hypothesis is false, why is the whole statement true and not undecided?

Let's take a hypothetical example: if I stay in the shower five more minutes, then I'll miss my bus.

I might miss my bus for any number of reasons: I can't find a textbook even though it was right there by the door; I discover a button missing right in the middle of my shirt; the cat makes a mess that I have to clean up before leaving the house; or maybe I trip and fall and twist an ankle on the way to the bus. Regardless, staying in the shower those extra five minutes would definitely make me miss my bus.

"I stay in the shower five more minutes" is p; "I'll miss my bus" is q. We know p can be either true or false, and the same for q, so here are the possible scenarios:

	p	q
1.	T	T
2.	T	F
3.	F	T
4.	F	F

Case 1 is pretty clear: p is true, and q is true, so the statement "if p, then q" is true. I stay in the shower five more minutes, and I miss my bus.

	p	q	$p \rightarrow q$
1.	T	T	T

Case 2 is also clear: p is true, and q is not true, so the statement "if p, then q" is false. I stay in the shower five more minutes, but the bus is late, too, so I make it.

	p	q	$p \rightarrow q$
1.	T	T	T
2.	T	F	F

Cases 3 and 4 are much more difficult to see. When p is not true, q can be anything it wants to be, and the statement will be true. The hypothesis is false, so the conclusion doesn't matter. This is where I trip and fall on the way to the bus, despite having gotten out of the shower on time. Maybe the bus is also late, or maybe not; it doesn't matter, because I didn't stay in the shower.

	p	*q*	*p* → *q*
1.	T	T	T
2.	T	F	F
3.	F	T	T
4.	F	F	T

A conditional statement doesn't mean the hypothesis or conclusion is true; it means that if the hypothesis is true, then the conclusion follows—it is also true. It doesn't say anything about the truth of the conclusion when the hypothesis is false. So the only way a conditional statement can be false is if the conclusion does not follow from the hypothesis.

—Dr. Math, The Math Forum

How do all of those statements about logic help us explain some of the geometry that we are learning? We can use the ideas in logic to help us make arguments that will convince other people that our geometric statements about the relationships between different objects are actually true. "Proofs" usually take one of two forms. The most common is the "paragraph proof," in which you present your argument in paragraph form (though it may take you more than one paragraph!). One form that is commonly taught in geometry courses is the "two-column proof." This consists of the same math you would use in a paragraph proof but reinforces the idea that each statement you make must have a reason behind it. We'll look at both kinds in this section.

What Are Proofs?

Dear Dr. Math,

I do not understand proofs. Can you help me out?

Yours truly,

Quentin

Hi, Quentin,

The study of geometry is the first place I encountered an axiom system. You start with certain "undefined objects," in this case, point, line, plane, and so on. Then you are given certain statements about them to accept as true. These are called postulates or **axioms**. They probably appear in the very first part of your textbook on Euclidean plane geometry. Examples might be

Any two distinct points lie on one and only one line.

Any two lines contain at most one common point.

Given a line and a point not on it, there is one and only one line not intersecting the given line and containing the given point.

The idea is to develop as many true statements (called theorems) as you can about points, lines, and so on, from these few postulates by using logical reasoning. A proof is a detailed description of the logical reasoning used to deduce a theorem from either the postulates or other previously proven theorems.

Along the way, more objects will be defined in terms of the original undefined objects, such as an angle, a line segment, a triangle, a circle, and so on. Theorems about these new objects are also deduced in the same way.

The first theorems you prove from the postulates are very simple statements. Using them, you prove more and more complicated theorems, including the Pythagorean theorem (the sum of the squares of the lengths of the legs of a right triangle equals the square of the length of the hypotenuse) and the one that says the sum of the measures of the interior angles in a triangle is 180 degrees.

One confusing thing about geometry proofs is that there is no single correct answer. Any logical sequence of true statements that ends with the desired theorem is a valid proof. There are always many correct proofs of any theorem. Some are shorter and simpler than others, and those are usually preferred by teachers, students, and mathematicians. Some are clever, some are tedious, and some are even considered beautiful or elegant. (I'll bet you didn't think that aesthetics could enter into mathematics, but it definitely does!)

Often proofs are constructed by working backward. Starting with the desired conclusion t, you could say, "If I could prove statement a, then using previously proved theorem (or postulate) b, I could conclude that t is true." This reduces your proof to proving statement a, then saying at the end of that proof, "Using theorem b, t is true." Often there are many possibilities for a (and b). The trick is to pick one that you can prove! Often several plausible choices for a (and b) are tried to find one that works (for you).

Some useful hints: Carefully review the hypothesis and conclusion of the theorem you want to prove. Keep in mind the postulates and previously proved theorems that might apply to the situation at hand. Consider working backward, as described earlier. Draw a figure (or several) to illustrate the situation. Consider constructing useful lines, points, circles, and so on.

—*Dr. Math, The Math Forum*

Two-Column Proofs

Dear Dr. Math,

I am having a real problem with proofs. In particular, two-column proofs. Can you explain the steps to prove geometric figures? I don't know how to word this any better, so I hope you can figure out what information I am trying to get.

Yours truly,

Qian

Hi, Qian,

A proof is meant to take the reader from a hypothesis to a conclusion, showing why we should have no doubt of the truth.

Hypothesis: if segments *AB* and *DE* intersect,

Conclusion: then the vertical angles (∠x and ∠y, ∠w and ∠z) formed by the intersection are equal.

After stating the hypothesis, begin building your proof with what you know. Usually there are some conditions that are given or there are some basic postulates on which you can rely.

The proof is built like a kind of scaffolding: once you state a premise and show why that's true, then you can confidently make another assertion supported by the previous premise.

With a two-column proof, you write what you know on the left side, and on the right side you say how you know that. The difficulty with two-column proofs often seems to revolve around how people organize their thinking, and the two-column proof does not fit with the way many of us think. Instead, it only serves to confuse our thinking. If this is the case, then one solution is to first sketch out the proof in your own words, then put it into the two-column format.

Another common difficulty is that the steps may seem so obvious that it's hard to know what is needed for a proof or why a proof is needed. Take our vertical angle example. This is something with which we are so familiar that it may be hard for us to recover the proof that we've already done in our heads long ago. When you can't figure out what needs to be said, it often helps to start speaking out loud and ask yourself after each statement you make: "how do you know?"

"It's obvious that the angles are equal."

"Yes. How do you know?"

"Because $\angle x$ and $\angle z$ make up a straight line and so do $\angle w$ and $\angle y$."

"Right, so how do you know $\angle x$ and $\angle y$ are equal?"

"If $\angle x$ and $\angle z$ are the same as $\angle y$ and $\angle z$, then take $\angle z$ away and you're left with $\angle x$ equals $\angle y$."

"Great! That's a proof. Now you just have to write it out in two columns."

AB intersects *DE*, forming vertical $\angle x$ and $\angle y$, $\angle z$ and $\angle w$	Hypothesis
1. $m\angle x + m\angle z = 180$ degrees	1. Definition of supplementary
2. $m\angle y + m\angle z = 180$ degrees	2. Definition of supplementary
3. $m\angle x + m\angle z = m\angle y + m\angle z$	3. Substitution
4. $m\angle x = m\angle y$	4. Subtraction
5. $m\angle x \cong m\angle z$	5. Definition of angle congruence

—*Dr. Math, The Math Forum*

Dear Dr. Math,

My geometry book only describes the two-column proof twice, and it doesn't give too many details. I cannot figure out if the statements and reasons are completely random in their ordering (other than the "given" and the "to prove," which are always first and last) or if there is a particular method for the order in which they should be placed.

   Figuring out which theorems, postulates, and definitions to use in a proof is no problem. However, the book never describes how the order of statements is chosen.

Yours truly,

Quentin

Hi, Quentin,

The only requirement for ordering the steps and reasons is that if step A depends on step B, then A should follow B. That is why the given is first and the conclusion is last, and the same logic applies to all intermediate steps.

   For example, prove: in triangle ABC, if side CA = side CB, then $\angle A \cong \angle B$.

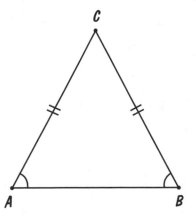

Proof

Steps	Reasons
1. $CA = CB$	1. Given
2. $CB = CA$	2. Step 1 and symmetric law of equality
3. $\angle C \cong \angle C$	3. Reflexive law of congruence
4. Triangle BCA $\cong$ triangle ACB	4. Steps 1, 2, 3, and the SAS theorem (which you'll learn about in part 3—it says if you know that two sides and the angle between them are congruent in two triangles, the triangles are congruent)
5. $\angle A \cong \angle B$	5. Step 4 and corresponding parts of congruent figures are congruent
Q.E.D.	

(Q.E.D. is an optional ending to proofs. It stands for *quod erat demonstrandum*, which is Latin for "that which was to be proved." It indicates the end of the proof, like "the end" in stories.)

In this proof, step 2 depends on step 1, so it must follow step 1. Step 4 depends on steps 1, 2, and 3, so it must follow them. Step 5 depends on step 4, so it must follow step 4. The only freedom you have is the placement of step 3, which can go anywhere before step 4 (just remember to renumber the steps and reasons to be in order 1 through 5).

Here is a diagram of the structure of the proof:

$$1 \Longrightarrow 2 \Longrightarrow 4$$

$$1 \Longrightarrow 4 \Longrightarrow 5$$

$$3 \Longrightarrow 4$$

The hard part is usually not figuring the order of the steps—it is figuring what steps are good ones to take! Usually the mathematician does this kind of thing backward (yes, backward!). He or she says, "If

I could prove that triangles *BCA* and *ACB* are congruent, then I could conclude that $\angle A \cong \angle B$ in one step. Furthermore, it seems from my diagram that this is probably true." So the mathematician tries to prove triangle congruence. "If I could find two sides and an included angle in *BCA* equal to two sides and an included angle in *ACB*, I could use side-angle-side to prove the triangles congruent." (You'll learn about side-angle-side, or SAS, in part 3.) So the mathematician hunts for equal sides and angles. When done, the proof is presented in the forward manner, not providing a hint of the backward process used to generate it. Sometimes you can work from the given forward and from the conclusion backward and meet somewhere in the middle.

—*Dr. Math, The Math Forum*

Dear Dr. Math,

How do you know what statement to write next when you're doing a proof? And what are the reasons that you use? For example, if I'm given $m\angle 4 + m\angle 6 = 180$, how do I prove $m\angle 5 = m\angle 6$?

Yours truly,

Qian

Hi, Qian,

Probably the most difficult part of proving something is deciding where to start. It takes a lot of practice, as well as trial and error. Since you are more interested in the thought process than the solution, let me tell you what went through my mind as I solved your example.

> Well, I don't need to know anything about the lengths of the triangle, because all I've been given are angles. I remember that the sum of the angles of a triangle is always 180 degrees, but that doesn't help, because I don't know what angle 5 is nor do I know what $m\angle JKL$ is. I know that $m\angle 4 + m\angle 6 = 180$. Ah! But I also know that $m\angle 4 + m\angle 5 = 180$, because together they form the straight line that contains JL. So if $m\angle 4 + m\angle 6 = 180 = m\angle 4 + m\angle 5$, then $m\angle 4 + m\angle 6 = m\angle 4 + m\angle 5$, and once we subtract $m\angle 4$ from both sides of this equation, we get our result, $m\angle 6 = m\angle 5$, so $\angle 6 \cong \angle 5$.

Notice that I tried to focus on the relevant parts of the problem based on what I was given (and importantly, what I was not given). I then relied on previous theorems or things I already knew that were relevant. I applied what I was given in the problem to this previous knowledge, and I was able to determine that some of my ideas didn't work. Luckily, I recognized that I could apply one of my ideas to the solution, and at that point I was able to see that this was the right direction to take. The rest was a matter of finishing the details.

While this is not always how proofs are made, it gives you an idea of the process, which is more or less educated trial and error. You guess, eliminate possibilities, and push the line of reasoning further. Some proofs like this one only require one breakthrough idea—namely, the fact that supplementary angles add up to 180 degrees. However, some proofs require applying many ideas, all in the right order. That's why they're difficult, because at each point in the proof there are many directions to take. Knowing which is the right one is something that takes practice and patience.

—Dr. Math, The Math Forum

Building a Geometric Proof

Dear Dr. Math,

I'm given that triangle *ABC* is a right triangle, with right angle at *C*. How do I prove that ∠*A* and ∠*B* are complementary angles?

I know to start like this, but I'm not sure what to do next.

Statement	Reason
Triangle *ABC* is a right triangle with angle at *C*	Given

Yours truly,

Quentin

Hi, Quentin,

Proofs are probably pretty new to you, and it does take time to get a feel for what makes a proof good enough and how you can find the way to prove something. It's really more like writing an essay than like doing the math you've done before—more creative and less mechanical. That makes it harder but also more rewarding and even fun.

One thing that's important is not to sit staring at an empty two-column chart. Our goal is to make a proof, not to fill in two columns; if we think about the columns too early, it can keep us from the goal.

I like to think of a proof as a bridge, or maybe a path through a forest: You have to start with some given facts and find a way to your destination. You have to start out by looking over the territory, getting a feel for where you are and where you have to go—what direction you have to head in, what landmarks you might find on the way, and how you'll know when you're getting close.

In this case, we start with a right triangle. Let's draw a diagram to see what we have:

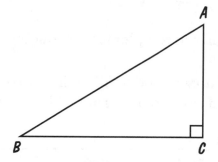

We have the structure built on one shore of the "river" we want to cross:

Statement	Reason
Triangle ABC is a right triangle with right angle at C	Given

We also know where we want to end up:

Statement	Reason
$\angle A$ and $\angle B$ are complementary angles	?

Let's look around a bit. What does "complementary" mean? It means that m$\angle A$ + m$\angle B$ = 90 degrees. That tells us we want to work with the angles of this triangle. What do we know about angles of a triangle? You may have several theorems to consider; one that should come to mind quickly is that the sum of the angles is 180 degrees.

What I've been doing here is looking at the tools and materials I have to build our bridge or path. So far I know I start with a triangle, one of whose angles is known; I want to get an equation involving the other two angles; and I have a theorem about all the angles of a triangle. That sounds promising!

Let's lay out what we have as the beginning of a proof:

Statement	Reason
Triangle ABC is a right triangle with right angle at C	Given
$A + B + C = 180$	Sum of angles theorem
$\angle A$ and $\angle B$ are complementary angles	?

What do we need to fill in the gaps? Let's rewrite the other statements in a way that looks more like the theorem we hope we can use:

Statement	Reason
Triangle ABC is a right triangle with right angle at C	Given
$\angle C = 90$	Definition of right angle
$\angle A + \angle B + \angle C = 180$	Sum of angles theorem
$\angle A + \angle B = 90$	?
$\angle A$ and $\angle B$ are complementary angles	Definition of complementary

Do you see how we're working both forward and backward? That's where my bridge-building analogy comes in: you can work on both ends of a bridge and let them meet in the middle.

How can we show that $\angle A + \angle B = 90$? Since $\angle C$ is 90, we can just do some algebra, subtracting the equation $\angle C = 90$ from $\angle A + \angle B + \angle C = 180$. You've done the same sort of thing in algebra without having to write it as a two-column proof; here we have to be able to say briefly why this works, and you may have been given a list of basic facts about algebra that you can use as reasons. I'll just call it "subtracting equals from equals."

All that's left is to put it together into a coherent proof. That means we have to figure out how to state each step clearly; each step has to follow from the steps that have already been written; and each step has to be small enough that we can give the reason without any huge leaps that would be hard to explain. Let's try:

Statement	Reason
1. Triangle ABC is a right triangle with right angle at C	1. Given
2. $\angle C = 90$	2. Definition of right angle
3. $\angle A + \angle B + \angle C = 180$	3. Sum of angles theorem
4. $\angle A + \angle B = 90$	4. Subtracting equals from equals
5. $\angle A$ and $\angle B$ are complementary angles	5. Definition of complementary

This proof could use some rewriting to make it clearer, and you should use the correct symbols for "the measure of $\angle C$" rather than just saying "C;" but it does the job. You should make those "cosmetic" improvements before you hand in your work.

A lot of students worry whether they have stated their reasons clearly, and usually most of the worries are about the most trivial steps—the facts we may not even be able to name because they're obvious. That's why texts often spend a lot of time labeling obvious facts, like "the reflexive property of equality"—not because they're really important but because the two-column format requires you to say something, and they don't want you to agonize over the wording. Real mathematicians don't worry about such details, as long as they know each step is true. The important thing is that you found a path. That's something to celebrate.

—*Dr. Math, The Math Forum*

Dear Dr. Math,

I was wondering if there is any way that you could break down the steps in doing a two-column proof? One that we had to do for homework is

Given: If ∠1 is congruent to ∠2 and ∠3 is congruent to ∠4,

Prove: n is parallel to p

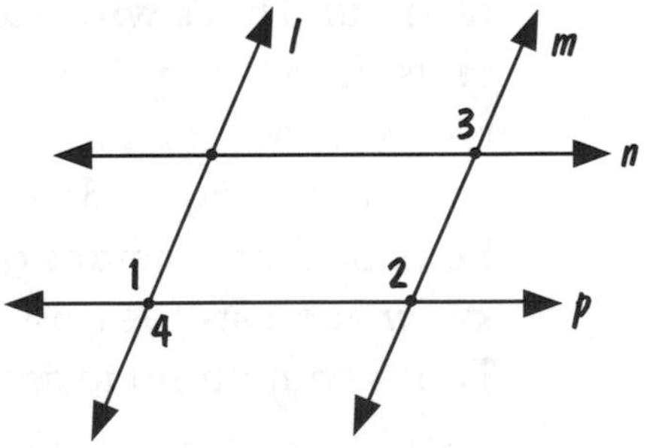

Yours truly,

Qian

Hi, Qian,

Two-column proofs are a little foreign to most of us—even to mathematicians, who don't usually use such a rigid way of writing a proof once they have learned what it means to prove something. The idea is to force you to think very clearly and express yourself very precisely. Unfortunately, no one really thinks that way, so if you're just shown a two-column proof without an explanation of how someone produced it, it seems like either magic ("How did he do that?") or a waste of time ("Why did he bother to do all that?").

I suggest that first you try to prove your goal without thinking about the details of the two columns. Too often people get bogged down in the details ("What is the exact reason for this step?" "Is this legal?") when the important thing about a proof is to learn the logic behind it.

A proof is sort of a bridge from the "mainland" of known truth to an "island" you want to get to. In your case, you have been given a platform you are supposed to start from (the "givens"), and you have some set of definitions, postulates, and already-proven theorems that you can use. Think of those as materials you can use to build the bridge:

Given: If ∠1 is congruent to ∠2 and ∠3 is congruent to ∠4,

Prove: *n* is parallel to *p*

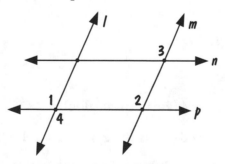

Now you need to take a quick helicopter ride over the territory between the starting and ending points and see what you can recognize as useful stepping-stones. It will take some practice to get used to what sorts of things you should look for. Just make a list of facts that you can either deduce from the givens or use to get to the goal. This is like building a bridge by starting at both ends and working toward the middle:

Given:

$\angle 1 = \angle 2$

$\angle 3 = \angle 4$

Deductions (from the givens):

$\angle 1 = \angle 4$ (vertical angles)

$\angle 1 = \angle 2$ implies that l and m are parallel.

Possibilities (for proving the goal):

n is parallel to p if $\angle 2$ and $\angle 3$ are equal.

Aha! I found a link.

I have $\angle 2 = \angle 1$ and $\angle 1 = \angle 4$ and $\angle 4 = \angle 3$, so I can prove that $\angle 2 = \angle 3$.

(Notice that I don't need all of my deductions.)

Now you have the idea of a proof, and you can start working out the details. We can locate the stepping-stones that our bridge will use:

Given:

$\angle 1 = \angle 2$

$\angle 3 = \angle 4$

Steps:

$\angle 1 = \angle 4$ (vertical angles)

$\angle 2 = \angle 3$ (because $\angle 2 = \angle 1 = \angle 4 = \angle 3$)

n is parallel to p (because $\angle 2 = \angle 3$)

It's starting to look like a proof. But now we need to organize it by stating clearly just what the reason is for each step—laying boards between the stepping-stones—and filling in some steps that help clarify what we are doing:

Given:

$\angle 1 \cong \angle 2$

$\angle 3 \cong \angle 4$

Statement	Reason
1. $\angle 1 \cong \angle 4$	1. Vertical angles are equal
2. $\angle 1 \cong \angle 2$	2. Given
3. $\angle 2 \cong \angle 4$	3. Both equal to $\angle 1$
4. $\angle 3 \cong \angle 4$	4. Given
5. $\angle 2 \cong \angle 3$	5. Both equal to $\angle 4$
6. Line n is parallel to p	6. Transversal makes equal angles

The exact wording will depend on what your text gives as the names of the theorems you use, how your teacher asks you to lay out the proof, and so on. That isn't the important thing, and you should not worry about the "rivets" in your proof (as long as they pass the teacher's inspection). Think about it. You've just built a bridge to new territory. When you get further, you'll have much more significant proofs to write. None of them will be a Golden Gate, but some will be pretty impressive. Right now, you're just hopping a puddle. It might not look like much, but it's good practice for building the big bridges.

—*Dr. Math, The Math Forum*

Indirect Proof

Many of the proofs that you have written are "direct" proofs, meaning that if whatever you want to prove is true, you go straight ahead and show that it is. But sometimes that's hard to do, because you're not really sure how to show it's true. That's where an "indirect" proof might be helpful. Using this strategy, you assume that what you want to prove is *not* true. Then you attempt to prove that your new statement is true. But if you can come up with a contradiction, then your original statement *is* true! This will make more sense when you look at some examples.

Are Tangents Perpendicular to the Radius of the Circle?

Dear Dr. Math,

I am supposed to prove that a line that is tangent to a circle is perpendicular to the radius drawn to the point of tangency. How do I do this?

Yours truly,

Quentin

Dear Quentin,

Here's a terminology check before we begin: a **tangent** is a line that touches a curve or a circle at a single point. (You could also have a plane tangent to a sphere: they meet at a single point as well.)

Let's say that the tangent line is *not* perpendicular to the radius. I know that's the opposite of what you're trying to prove, but stick with me.

If *BA* isn't perpendicular to *j*, then there has to be another segment through *B*, such as *BC*, which is perpendicular. Since the perpendicular segment from a point to a line is the shortest segment from a point to a line, *BC* is shorter than *BA*. But this is a contradiction! We know that *BA* is shorter than *BC*, because *C* is outside the circle, but *A* is on the circle. So *A* has to be closer to *B* than *C*.

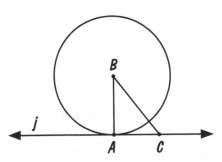

This contradiction means that our "opposite" statement—that *j* is not perpendicular to *BA*—must be false. So we know that *j* is perpendicular to *BA*, which is what you wanted to prove in the first place.

—*Dr. Math, The Math Forum*

Dear Dr. Math,

I am really having trouble with this "converse proof" question. Here's what I have to do: "Use the following diagram to prove the converse of the parallel lines theorem: if a transversal intersects two lines so that the alternate angles are equal, then the lines are parallel."

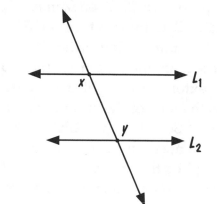

Given: m∠x = m∠y

Prove: L_1 is parallel to L_2

We are to assume that the theorem is incorrect (in this case, the angles are not equal) and disprove the assumption, therefore proving the theorem is correct.

Another question I am having trouble with is the following: "In triangle *DEF*, *G* and *H* are the midpoints of *DE* and *DF*, respectively. The line segments *EH* and *FG* are medians. Prove that these medians cannot bisect each other."

Unfortunately, all that the answer part of my text says is "answers may vary." Please help!

Yours truly,

Qian

Hi, Qian,

Let's work through this. You'll notice that your description of what you have to do was a little off; you have to assume the conclusion is false and prove that the given must be false.

Given: $m\angle x = m\angle y$

Prove: $L_1 \parallel L_2$

Assume that the conclusion is false: L_1 is *not* parallel to L_2. Then L_1 meets L_2 at some point C, forming a triangle ABC.

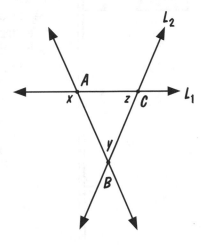

What contradiction arises? Here's one: there's another theorem that says that an exterior angle of a triangle is equal to the sum of the two remote interior angles. So in triangle ABC, we know that $m\angle x = m\angle y + m\angle z$. But since $m\angle z > 0$, this implies that $m\angle x$ is not equal to $m\angle y$ and therefore that they are not congruent. This contradiction proves the theorem.

The details will depend on what theorems you have available; if they haven't proved the external angle theorem I used, then there will be something similar you can use in its place. But however you fill in the details, the idea is to draw a (wrong) diagram in which the conclusion is false, then use it to prove the premises are false.

Let's look at your second problem:

In triangle DEF, G and H are the midpoints of DE and DF, respectively. The line segments EH and FG are medians. Prove that these medians cannot bisect each other.

(Remember that medians are segments from each vertex to the midpoint of the opposite side.) Here's my attempt at a diagram:

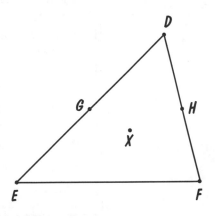

This sounds odd to me, because I know a theorem that says the medians divide one another in the ratio 1:2, so I could just state that theorem, then say 1:2 is not that same as 1:1, so it doesn't bisect. Given that, this is a silly theorem, since there's a much stronger positive statement to be made. I'll assume you haven't learned that yet, so you can't use it.

In that case, this sounds like a time to use proof by contradiction again, since the conclusion has a negative form. Let's suppose that *EH* and *FG* intersect at point *X*, which is their midpoint. Then *EX* = *XH*. What can we look for that would lead to a contradiction with the assumption that *G* and *H* are midpoints of *DE* and *DF*?

I look at the figure and recognize that *GH* is parallel to *EF*, and alternate interior angles tell me that *GHX* and *FEX* are similar

I'm beginning to see the logic behind proofs.

Yeah. We just have to remember to give reasons for the steps that we've been taking all along, and we should be fine.

triangles. But if $EX = XH$, then they are actually congruent triangles! See if you can use that to complete the proof. Or, you might find that you can rework this as a direct proof that $EX > XH$. But if you do well, you'll find that it actually proves $EX = 2XH$—the theorem I mentioned before.

—*Dr. Math, The Math Forum*

Resources on the Web

Learn more about logic and proof at these sites:

Math Forum: Geometry Problem of the Week: Angle Trisection with a Carpenter's Square

mathforum.org/geopow/solutions/solution.ehtml?puzzle=218

Prove how a carpenter's square can be used to trisect an angle.

Math Forum: Geometry Problem of the Week: Proofs Without Words

mathforum.org/geopow/archive/solutio86.html

Drawings can prove mathematical statements. What picture would prove what $(a + b)^2$ is equal to? How about $(a + b)(c + d)$?

Math Forum: Geometry Problem of the Week: Proofs Without Words II

mathforum.org/geopow/solutions/solution.ehtml?puzzle=6

Based on a simple example that illustrates the distributive property, explain what the second picture illustrates.

Shodor Organization: Project Interactivate: Squaring the Triangle

shodor.org/interactivate/activities/pyth/index.html

Students learn how the Pythagorean theorem works through investigating the standard geometric proof.

PART 3

Triangles: Properties, Congruence, and Similarity

Much of your study of triangles up to this point has involved identifying the different types, then using properties of those types to solve problems. We did a lot of that with you in our previous book, *Dr. Math Introduces Geometry*. In this part, we'll talk about the triangle inequality property, which is used in surprisingly large

I thought we learned a lot about triangles in middle school.

We did, but just like with other topics in math that we started learning about when we were younger, we're learning even more now!

numbers of geometry problems, as well as definitions and properties of the centers of triangles. We'll also talk about how to prove when triangles are congruent and similar.

In this part, Dr. Math explains

- the triangle inequality property
- centers of triangles
- isosceles and equilateral triangles
- congruence in triangles: SSS, SAS, and ASA
- similarity in triangles
- congruence proofs

The Triangle Inequality Property

The triangle inequality property explains why any three sides do not always make a triangle. The sides have to *reach*—that is, they have to be long enough to form a two-dimensional figure.

Triangle Perimeter

Dear Dr. Math,
How many triangles have sides whose lengths total 15 units?
Yours truly,
Qian

Hi, Qian,

There are many kinds of answers for your question. Do you mean that the lengths of the triangle's sides must be whole numbers, or might they be real numbers (that is, decimals or fractions)? In the former case, there is only a limited number of possibilities—seven, in fact (see the following page)—whereas in the latter case, there is an infinite number of answers.

Let's take a simple example. If we had two sides of 7 units each, the third side would be 1 unit. This is a very narrow isosceles triangle, resembling a sharp-pointed knife. But we could also imagine another triangle, also isosceles, with these side lengths: 7.1, 7.1, and 0.8. Or another: 7.05, 7.05, and 0.9. Or another: 6.9, 6.9, and 1.2. And those are just some isosceles versions. We could also form a scalene triangle like this: 7.1, 7.0, and 0.9. When we begin admitting number values such as these, it begins to be clear that there are many ways to do it.

To see this, take a loop of string of length 15 units and note that you can form many nonsimilar triangles out of it by holding three fingers in the loop and pulling taut. If we limit ourselves to positive integer values, however, the story changes considerably. Essentially we need to find out how many solutions there are for this equation:

$$a + b + c = 15$$

where a, b, and/or c may be distinct values or even equal to one another. One solution $(7, 7, 1)$ was just discussed. But even this is not quite enough. You see, $(2, 5, 8)$ would be another solution to the equation, but you couldn't form a triangle with those lengths. With 8 as one side, the two sides of 2 and 5 (whose sum is 7) wouldn't "meet" or connect.

So we need to add one more fact to our search, called the triangle inequality property. This says that in any triangle, the sum of the lengths of any two sides must exceed the length of the third side. In our good example, we have $7 + 1 > 7$; but in our bad example, we have $2 + 5 < 8$.

With a little patience, we can systematically form a list of solutions:

1. 1-7-7
2. 2-6-7
3. 3-6-6
4. 3-5-7
5. 4-4-7
6. 4-5-6
7. 5-5-5

Note how we let a equal the smallest side and kept it constant as long as possible while looking for the lengths of b and c. This is just to get organized. If you are concerned about obtaining all the solutions, it helps to have a systematic way of searching for them, such as letting a be the length of the smallest side.

—*Dr. Math, The Math Forum*

Centers of Triangles

When you talk about the center of a circle, there is only one possible point. If you're talking about centers of other objects, it's often a bit more complicated. How do you find the center of your backyard, for example? It certainly depends on what shape the yard is! In this section, we'll look at the different types of centers of triangles.

Proofs with Isosceles Triangles

Dear Dr. Math,

I don't understand the difference between angle bisectors, medians, and altitudes. Here's a problem that I have to prove:

In an isosceles triangle, the altitude is a median and an angle bisector.

I know that *BD* is an altitude of triangle *ABC*, but I need to prove why it's also a median and an angle bisector. This is where I get really lost. Please help.

Yours truly,
Quentin

Hi, Quentin,

To understand what facts we are given and what we need to prove, let's review some definitions. The altitude, median, and angle bisector of a triangle are all line segments that join one vertex of a triangle to the opposite side. (In some cases, the side may have to be extended beyond a vertex.)

The **altitude** is perpendicular to that opposite side.

The **median** meets the opposite side at the midpoint of the side.

The **angle bisector** bisects, or divides in half, the angle of the triangle at the vertex.

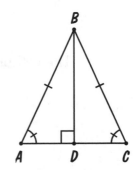

To answer the question, we can construct the altitude from *B*. This will be perpendicular to *AC* by definition. Because triangle *ABC* is isosceles, you also know that *AB* and *BC* are equal (and by the theorem that says the base angles of an isosceles triangle are equal, so angles *BAC* and *BCA* are equal).

You need to prove that

1. *AD* = *DC* (so *BD* is a median)

2. ∠*ABD* = ∠*DBC* (so *BD* is an angle bisector)

Can you do the proof now that we have spelled out what you start with and what you need to prove? Try it. (Hint: see if you can find congruent triangles.)

—*Dr. Math, The Math Forum*

Orthocenter, Circumcenter, and Centroid

Dear Dr. Math,

I have been having trouble finding the Euler line on a triangle. If you would explain to me, I would be most grateful!

Yours truly,

Qian

Hi, Qian,

The **Euler line** of a triangle is the line that passes through the ortho-center, circumcenter, and centroid of the triangle.

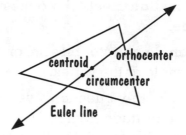

The **orthocenter** is the intersection of the triangle's altitudes.

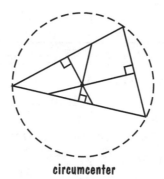

orthocenter

The **circumcenter** is the intersection of the perpendicular bisec-tors of the three sides. (A **perpendicular bisector** divides a line seg-ment in half and meets the segment at right angles.) It is called the "circumcenter" because it is also the center of the **circumscribed circle** (a circle drawn around the triangle that goes through the tri-angle's vertices).

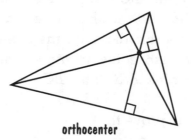

circumcenter

The **centroid** is the intersection of the three medians of the triangle.

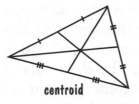

centroid

It's pretty neat that those three points are always on the same line!

—*Dr. Math, The Math Forum*

<table>
<tr><td>

The Angle Bisectors of a Triangle

</td><td>

Dear Dr. Math,

In a triangle, the bisectors of the angles intersect at a point in the interior of the circle. If I use this point as a center to draw a circle, what is the relation of this circle to the triangle?

Please help me with the answer. Thank you.

Yours truly,

Quentin

</td></tr>
</table>

Hi, Quentin,

This question uses the following: the bisector of an angle is the locus of points that have equal distances to the legs of the triangle. For instance, any point on the angle bisector of angle A in the diagram below is as far from AB as it is from AC.

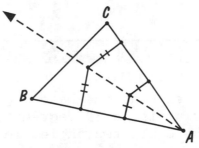

The point where all of the angle bisectors meet is called the **incenter**, which we'll call I. This point is on all three of the angle bisectors, and thus its distances to the sides of ABC are all equal.

You asked what happens if you use this point as the center of a circle and how that circle is related to the triangle. You can draw lots of circles with their center at *I*, but the one that you're probably most interested in is the incircle, which is a circle centered at *I* that is tangent to all three sides of the triangle.

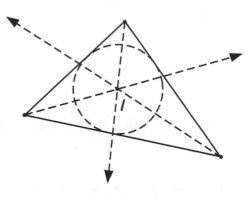

—Dr. Math, The Math Forum

Isosceles and Equilateral Triangles

Isosceles and equilateral triangles have special properties, which means that we can figure out more about them than we might about a scalene triangle. An **isosceles triangle** has at least two equal sides. They're usually called the **legs**, while the third side is called the **base**. The two base angles—those that include the base of the triangle—are equal.

In an **equilateral triangle**, all of the sides and the angles are equal. An equilateral triangle is also an isosceles triangle, so everything that is true about isosceles triangles is also true of equilateral triangles.

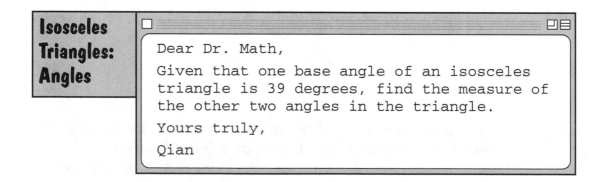

Isosceles Triangles: Angles

Dear Dr. Math,

Given that one base angle of an isosceles triangle is 39 degrees, find the measure of the other two angles in the triangle.

Yours truly,

Qian

Hi, Qian,

To start, let's make sure you understand the definitions of the terms.

> An isosceles triangle has two congruent sides with a third side that is the base.

> A base angle of an isosceles triangle is one of the angles formed by the base and another side. Base angles are equal because of the definition of an isosceles triangle.

A diagram would probably help here:

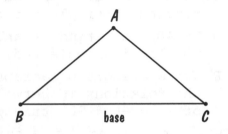

ABC is an isosceles triangle. AB is congruent to AC. ∠ABC is congruent to ∠ACB. These are the base angles. Now let's look at what we're given and what we're asked to find out.

We're given that one of the base angles is 39 degrees. We know that the base angles are congruent, so we actually know that both base angles are 39 degrees—that is, we know that ∠ABC and ∠ACB are both 39 degrees. We're asked to find out the measures of the other two angles, and we've found one of them already, so all we need to find out is the measure of ∠BAC.

$$m\angle ABC = m\angle ACB = 39 \text{ degrees}$$

$$m\angle BAC =$$

We know two out of the three angles, but we've used up the specific information we were given. Now we need to look for some general rule that will connect the unknown (∠BAC) to the known (∠ABC and ∠ACB). Do you know such a rule?

How about the sum of the angles in a triangle? If the two angles you have are correct, you should be able to subtract their sum from 180 degrees and find the answer you need.

—*Dr. Math, The Math Forum*

Dear Dr. Math,

Triangle *ABC* is equilateral, and *AD* is one of its heights.

A. Copy the figure and write the measures of all the acute angles on the figure.

B. Is angle *ADB* equal to angle *ADC*? Prove it.

C. If *AB* = 2, find *BD* and *AD*. Leave your results in simple radical form.

D. If *AB* = 10, find *BD* and *AD*. Leave your results in simple radical form.

E. Write a short paragraph that describes the relationship between the three sides of a 30°–60°–90° triangle.

Where do I start with this problem? Can you explain what simple radical form is and how to answer questions like this one in the future?

Yours truly,

Quentin

Hi, Quentin,

You should start by drawing a diagram of the triangle (as the question says to do).

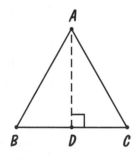

The most important thing to notice here is that triangle *ABC* is equilateral. An equilateral triangle is a triangle that has three equal angles and three equal sides. As you know, there are 180 degrees in a triangle. So if you have 180 degrees divided by three equal angles, each angle should be 60 degrees.

For part B, *ADB* and *ADC* are the two angles that are formed when the height *AD* touches the base *BC*. So what is a height, anyway? It's a line drawn from one of the angles of a triangle so that it is perpendicular to the side opposite the angle—that is, it forms a right angle with the opposite side.

For part C, take a look at triangle *ABD*. What do you know about this triangle? You know that *AB* = 2 and that ∠*ADB* is a right angle. You also know something about *BD*. Think about it. You have a triangle where all the sides are the same, and you are dividing it exactly in half with the height *AD*. So since all the sides are equal, meaning the whole side, *BC*, is 2, half of the side, *BD*, should just be 1.

Now you know two sides of a right triangle. How about using the Pythagorean theorem to find the other? You can probably think about part D in the same way.

For part E, this question is asking you to make some conclusions from what you learned about your triangle *ABD* in parts C and D. *ABD* is a 30°–60°–90° triangle (60 degrees for ∠*B*, 90 degrees for ∠*D*, and you are left with 30 degrees for ∠*A*). As it turns out, when you have a 30°–60°–90° triangle, there are certain relationships that always exist between the lengths of the three sides. Can you take a guess at these? Take a look at your answers from parts C and D. Notice, for

example, that the length of the hypotenuse (side *AB*) is twice the smallest side length (*BD*) in both cases. Another way to try to answer this question is to use variables in your side lengths. Set side *DB* equal to *x*. What do you know about the other side lengths? By using variables, you make sure the relations are the same for all triangles, not just the ones you are looking at. Don't forget that you can use the Pythagorean theorem with variables as well as with numbers.

—Dr. Math, The Math Forum

Congruence in Triangles: SSS, SAS, and ASA

When we say that two things are congruent, we mean that every part of one thing is the same as the corresponding part of the other thing. But to be able to prove that two triangles are congruent, we don't need to show that all of their corresponding parts (sides and angles) are equal. We can use some shortcuts so that we can get by with less information yet still know that the two triangles are the same in every way.

In this section, we'll explain how to use these shortcuts, or postulates: SSS (side-side-side), SAS (side-angle-side), and ASA (angle-side-angle). We'll also show you why SSA (side-side-angle) and AAA (angle-angle-angle) shortcuts won't work, at least most of the time.

Congruence and Triangles

Dear Dr. Math,

Can you please explain how to determine if a shape is congruent using SSS, SAS, and ASA and how and when to use the triangle congruence properties? I have tried, but I just don't understand it. Please start from the beginning. Thanks.

Yours truly,

Qian

Hi, Qian,

First of all, let us agree on the following four things:

1. Two line segments are congruent if and only if they have the same length. If we know that segments *FI* and *SE* are each 7.3 cm long, then segment *FI* is congruent to segment *SE*, which we can write as $FI \cong SE$.

2. Two angles are congruent if and only if they measure the same number of degrees. So if $\angle GUS$ and $\angle JON$ each measure 81 degrees, then $\angle GUS$ and $\angle JON$ are congruent.

3. Congruence of segments and angles is reflexive, transitive, and symmetric. **Reflexive** means segment *AB* is congruent to itself; transitive means if segment *CD* is congruent to segment *EF* and segment *EF* is congruent to segment *GH*, then segment *CD* is congruent to segment *GH*; and **symmetric** means if segment *IJ* is congruent to segment *KL*, then segment *KL* is congruent to segment *IJ*. The same holds true for angles.

4. Two triangles are congruent if and only if they have three pairs of congruent sides and three pairs of congruent angles. Triangle *ABC* and triangle *XYZ* are congruent if and only if $\angle A$ is congruent to $\angle X$, $\angle B$ is congruent to $\angle Y$, $\angle C$ is congruent to $\angle Z$, side *XY* is congruent to side *AB*, side *BC* is congruent to side *YZ*, and side *AC* is congruent to side *XZ*.

Note that when you say two triangles are congruent, you have to get the letters in the proper order to show what's congruent to what. If I had said triangle *BAC* was congruent to triangle *YXZ*, then that's okay (check it out). But if I say triangle *YZX* is congruent to triangle *CAB*, then that's wrong. (Why?)

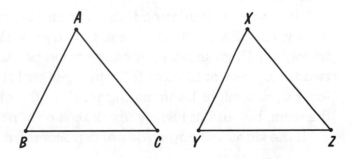

There are a lot of things that you have to check in that last one. Six pairs of things have to be congruent. Wow. Most of the time you don't have the luxury of having all that information. Are there any shortcuts?

It turns out that there are some shortcuts, and those are the SSS, SAS, and ASA postulates that you mentioned. SSS (the letters stand for "side-side-side") means that if you have two triangles and you can show that the three pairs of corresponding sides are congruent, then the two triangles are congruent. This is a postulate, not a theorem, meaning that it cannot be proved, but it appears to be true, so everybody accepts it. So if you have triangles *ANT* and *FLY* and you can show that *AN* = *FL*, *NT* = *LY*, and *AT* = *FY*, then the two triangles are congruent.

SAS (the letters stand for "side-angle-side") means that if you have triangles *BOY* and *GRL* and you can find two pairs of congruent corresponding sides *and* a pair of congruent corresponding angles *between* the two pairs of sides we just mentioned, then the two triangles are congruent. Again, this is a postulate. Suppose in triangles *BOY* and *GRL* we know that *BO* = *RL*, *BY* = *GR*, and $\angle B$ = $\angle R$. Then I can claim that triangle *BOY* is congruent to triangle *RLG* using the SAS postulate.

ASA (the letters stand for "angle-side-angle") means that if you have triangles *DOG* and *CAT* and you can find two pairs of congruent corresponding angles *and* a pair of congruent corresponding sides *between* the two pairs of angles we just mentioned, then the two triangles are congruent. Again, this is a postulate. Suppose in triangles *DOG* and *CAT* we know that $\angle D$ = $\angle T$, $\angle O$ = $\angle C$, and *DO* = *CT*. I claim that triangle *DOG* is congruent to triangle *TCA* using the *ASA* postulate.

You may be wondering if there is an SSA postulate. No, unfortunately, the SSA postulate doesn't always work, especially in acute triangles. There is no AAA congruence postulate either, since the two triangles would have the same general shape (that is, be similar) but one might be much bigger than the other. There is an AAS theorem, but let's not worry about that right now.

If the sides and angles do not correspond, there is no congruence.

For example, if we have triangle *NBC* and triangle *KLM* and ∠*N* = ∠*K*, ∠*B* = ∠*L*, and *KL* = *CN*, then those triangles are *not* necessarily congruent.

Here are four exercises for you to try. I suggest you draw a diagram for each one. (The answers are below. Hide them from yourself.)

1. In triangles *RUN* and *HID*, ∠*R* = ∠*D*, ∠*U* = ∠*I*, and *RU* = *DI*. What triangles are congruent, if any, and why?

2. In triangles *FRE* and *SLV*, *FR* = *LV*, *EF* = *SL*, and ∠*F* = ∠*S*. What triangles are congruent, if any, and why?

3. In triangles *MUS* and *CHR*, ∠*S* = ∠*H*, *US* = *HR*, and ∠*U* = ∠*R*. What triangles are congruent, if any, and why?

4. In triangles *QWE* and *RTY*, *QW* = *TY*, *WE* = *RY*, and *QE* = *RT*. What triangles are congruent, if any, and why?

Here are the answers:
1. Yes; triangle *RUN* ≅ triangle *DIH* by ASA.
2. No; the sides and angles do not match.
3. Yes; triangle *SUM* ≅ triangle *HRC* by ASA.
4. Yes; triangle *QWE* ≅ triangle *TYR* by SSS.

—*Dr. Math, The Math Forum*

More about Triangle Congruence

Dear Dr. Math,

I don't understand how to tell if two triangles are congruent. My teacher told me to use SSS (side-side-side), SAS (side-angle-side), and ASA (angle-side-angle) to figure out if they are congruent, but I don't understand.

I think it has something to do with seeing if all the sides and angles match up.

Yours truly,

Quentin

Hi, Quentin,

Suppose you wanted to tell if a twenty-dollar bill is genuine. You would compare it with a real one and see if everything is the same (except for serial numbers, which you can ignore). Is the number in the upper left printed the same way on both? Is the right ear in the portrait the same in both bills? And so on.

To see if two triangles are the same, or "congruent," you could do the same thing: match up and compare each part of one with the corresponding part from the other. (Are these angles the same? What about the side clockwise around from there?) Once you had compared every single part, you would know if they were congruent.

But we have several theorems (or postulates) that say we don't have to check every part; it's enough to check just three parts, if we choose the right three. Specifically, the following:

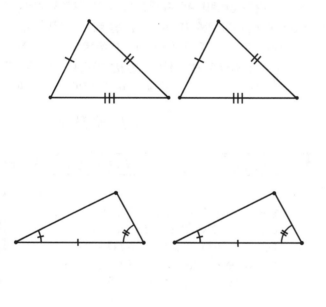

SSS tells us that if each side of one matches the corresponding side of the other, then the triangles are congruent.

ASA tells us that if two angles of one match the corresponding angles of the other and the sides between those angles match, then the triangles are congruent.

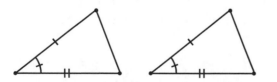

SAS tells us that if two sides of one match the corresponding sides of the other and the angles between them match, then the triangles are congruent.

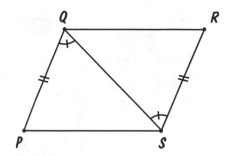

Now, it is not enough to say that a pair of angles *look* the same; you have to *know* they are. Typically in geometry proof, you are told (or know for other reasons) that certain parts are congruent. For example, you might be told in this figure that *PQ* is the same length as RS and ∠*PQS* has the same measure as *RSQ*. You know without having to be told that any segment is congruent to itself, so QS ≅ SQ.

So if we think about triangles *PQS* and *RSQ* (with the letters given in the order we want to compare them), we can turn the latter around in our minds so that they line up with the letters in corresponding spots like this:

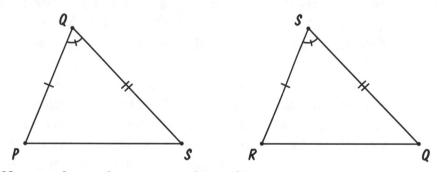

Now we have three pairs of matching parts:

$PQ \cong RS$

$\angle PQS \cong \angle RSQ$

$QS \cong SQ$

And these are in the order SAS, with the angle between the sides. So the SAS theorem tells us that the two triangles are congruent. We don't have to know anything about the other side and angles; it's like saying that if the left ears match, the right ears will match, too, so we don't need to check them.

—*Dr. Math, The Math Forum*

Dear Dr. Math,

Can you give me a construction to show that side-side-angle does not prove two triangles congruent? I thought it wasn't supposed to work, but for some reason I keep coming up with two congruent triangles when I am done. It would be great if I could do this using Geometer's Sketchpad.

Yours truly,

Qian

Hi, Qian,

For many combinations of side-side-angle, two triangles will be congruent. But there are instances when this isn't enough information to determine a unique triangle. There are some cases where the side, side, and angle describe two possible triangles!

Consider this: we have an angle of 30 degrees, a side of 6, and a side of 4, in that order. What will that triangle look like? Let's draw it. In the figure below, we start with the 30-degree angle and then go 6 units. From that point, which is the top of the triangle below, we're supposed to go 4 units to get back to the base of the triangle. But when we draw a circle with radius 4, it intersects the line in two different places!

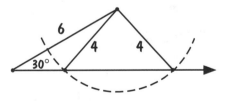

If you wanted to show this in a program like the Geometer's Sketchpad, you could set up something like the following: construct an angle with a measure of x degrees using two segments, and construct two separate segments j and k. These will be your angle, side, and side. You'll also need a ray upon which to build your triangle (the endpoint of my ray is point A and it's horizontal). You're going to end up with something like the following diagram:

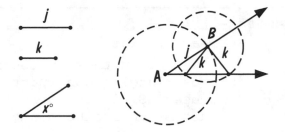

First, rotate your ray around A by x degrees. That's our angle. Next, construct a circle centered at A with radius j. Where that circle intersects the rotated ray is point B, which is j units away from A. That's our first side. Now from B, construct a circle with radius k. In the case above, this gives two different results. As you can see from the figures below, though, there are other possible solutions as well. In the first case, the circle centered at B only intersects the line at one point, as it's too big to hit twice. In the second case, it only intersects the line at one point, so the ray is tangent to the circle.

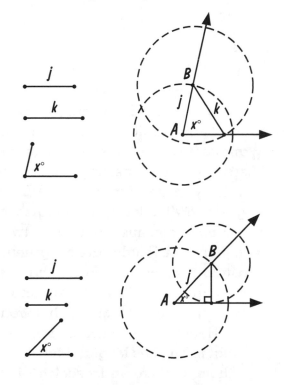

—Dr. Math, The Math Forum

Dear Dr. Math,

I was given these three methods of proving two triangles congruent: SSS, SAS, ASA. If I use SAS, is it correct that the angle must be an included angle?

Then, two triangles, one that has two sides of equal length to corresponding sides of the second triangle and both having an angle (not included) equal, cannot be proved congruent. It seems to me that they are congruent, though. Any thoughts on this?

Yours truly,

Quentin

Hi, Quentin,

If you use SAS, yes, the known angle must be included between the known sides: order matters.

As for your second question, what you are looking for is an SSA postulate. I am afraid that it just isn't there. It is interesting to see why, and there are a few special cases in which it actually works.

Let's look at one special case, then we'll look at a more general case. Are you familiar with the HL (hypotenuse-leg) postulate of congruence? It is for right triangles, and it says that if the corresponding hypotenuse and leg of two right triangles are congruent, then the triangles are congruent. That essentially is an SSA postulate, except we require that the A be a right angle. Requiring a right angle is pretty restrictive! But now, let's look at a less restricted triangle for which it won't work.

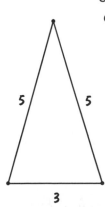

Here is an experiment for you to try. Get three sticks: one that is 3 inches long and two that are each 5 inches long. Use them to make an isosceles triangle. It will look something like the picture on the left.

Draw a diagram of the triangle you made and label the sides as on the previous page.

Now I want you to keep the angle fixed between the two 5-inch sticks and move the 3-inch stick in until it forms a triangle again.

If you have followed these instructions, you have constructed two triangles that have congruencies SSA but are clearly not congruent triangles.

—*Dr. Math, The Math Forum*

Two objects are **similar** if they are scale images of each other. For example, any two squares are similar—they have the same shape but not necessarily the same size. Any two triangles are similar if all three angles are equal and all three sides are in proportion. (Although if one is true, both must be true, as they imply each other: if the sides are in proportion, then the angles must be equal, and vice versa.) Instead of being congruent as in congruent triangles, the corresponding parts of similar triangles are in proportion. As with congruence, there are several shortcuts you can use to determine if two triangles are similar.

Prove Triangles Are Similar

> Dear Dr. Math,
> How do you prove two triangles to be similar?
> Yours truly,
> Qian

Hi, Qian,

You can tell if two triangles are similar in a lot of different ways, but all of them involve comparing sides and angles. If all of the sides of each triangle are in proportion to the corresponding sides in the other triangle, or if all of the angles are equal, then the triangles are similar. Also, since equal angles are opposite similar-length sides, you can prove that two triangles are similar when any of the following seven conditions are true:

1. If two sets of corresponding sides are in proportion and the angle between them is equal (SAS)

2. If two corresponding angles are equal and the side between them is in proportion (ASA)

3. If two angles are equal and another side is in proportion (AAS)

4. If, in a right triangle, the hypotenuse and one leg are both in proportion (HL)

5. If all three sides are in proportion (SSS)

6. If all three angles are equal (AAA)

7. If two sides are in proportion and one angle is equal (SSA)

You should also know that any of these *except* items 6 and 7 can be used to prove triangles congruent *if you change* proportionate sides for congruent ones.

—Dr. Math, The Math Forum

Measuring the Height of a Build-ing Using Shadows

Dear Dr. Math,

I have to write a shadow report for math, and I need to know what time of day is best to use a shadow to measure the height of a building or object with triangles. Please help with information on shadows and the best and worst times of day to find the size of a building. I'm also a little con-fused about how exactly to use shadows and triangles to find the size of a building.

Yours truly,

Quentin

Hi, Quentin,

One way to find the height of a build-ing makes use of similar triangles. Put a vertical post in the ground (or have someone hold it vertical) and measure its height and the length of its shadow. Measure the length of the building's shadow before the sun has time to move. Now you have two triangles with three known lengths:

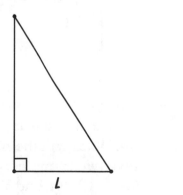

You know the height *h* and shadow length *l* of the post and the shadow length *L* of the building. The two triangles are similar. Why? From these facts you can find the height of the building.

Let's say it's near noon, so the shadows are very short. Perhaps a 30-foot building casts a 10-foot shadow. If your measurement of the length of the shadow is off by 1 foot, how far off will your estimate of the building's height be?

In contrast, what if the shadows are very long—the 30-foot building casts a shadow 90 feet long? If your measurement of the shadow is off by 1 foot, how far off will your estimate of the building's height be?

If you explore the questions above, a longer shadow is better than a short shadow. However, if the shadow of the building is a mile long when the sun has just risen, you'll have a problem measuring such a large distance. So you'll want to measure the shadow at a time when it's long enough to get a smaller margin of error but not so long that it's too difficult to measure.

—Dr. Math, The Math Forum

Turning a Perimeter into a Scale Factor

Dear Dr. Math,

Perimeter and area ratios of similar figures are given. Find each scale factor:

perimeter ratio = 81

scale factor = ?

Yours truly,

Qian

Hi, Qian,

Let's get at the idea by working backward. Suppose we know the **scale factor**, the amount of increase or decrease in the size of the figure. What will the ratio of perimeters be? For instance, suppose we have two triangles. One has sides of 3, 4, and 5 inches; the other has sides of 33, 44, and 55 inches. The scale factor is 11: you multiply each side length of the first triangle to get the corresponding side length of the second triangle.

Now look at the perimeters. The perimeter of the first triangle is $3 + 4 + 5 = 12$ inches. The perimeter of the second triangle is $33 + 44 + 55 = 132$ inches. The ratio of perimeters is $\frac{132}{12} = 11$. Do you notice that it's the same as the scale factor? This will always be true! Here's why. We can write the sides of the second triangle as $3 \cdot 11, 4 \cdot 11$, and $5 \cdot 11$. Then the perimeter is

$$3 \cdot 11 + 4 \cdot 11 + 5 \cdot 11 = (3 + 4 + 5) \cdot 11$$

using the distributive property. To find the ratio of perimeters, divide this by the perimeter of the first triangle:

$$\frac{(3 + 4 + 5) \cdot 11}{3 + 4 + 5} = 11$$

Let's continue and think about the ratio of areas. The triangles I chose happen to be right triangles (Do you know how to show this?), so the area is half the product of the two shorter sides. Thus the area of the first triangle is $\frac{3 \cdot 4}{2} = 6$ square inches. The area of the second triangle is $\frac{33 \cdot 44}{2} = 726$ square inches. The ratio of areas is $\frac{726}{6} = 121$. This ratio happens to be 11^2. It will always be true that the ratio of areas is the square of the scale factor.

Again, we can see why this is true. Writing the sides of the second triangle as $3 \cdot 11$ and $4 \cdot 11$, the area is

$$3 \cdot 11 \cdot 4 \cdot 11 = (3 \cdot 4)(11 \cdot 11)$$

Divide this by the area of the first triangle to find the ratio of areas:

$$\frac{(3 \cdot 4)(11 \cdot 11)}{3 \cdot 4} = 11 \cdot 11 = 121$$

Do you see how it works now? What is the answer to your problem?

—*Dr. Math, The Math Forum*

Congruence Proofs

We have learned some ways to show that triangles are congruent. But how would we use these postulates to determine that particular triangles actually are congruent or to show that specific angles or segments might be equal to each other?

<table>
<tr>
<td>

Corresponding Parts of Congruent Triangles Are Congruent (CPCTC)

</td>
<td>

Dear Dr. Math,

I am a freshman and my teacher taught us CPCTC, but I do not understand when to use it, why we use it, and how it proves any-thing. Can you help?

Yours truly,

Quentin

</td>
</tr>
</table>

Hi, Quentin,

CPCTC (corresponding congruent parts of congruent triangles are congruent) is a complicated way to say something obvious: if two things are identical, then every part of them is identical, too. For example, if I wrote you a letter and made a photocopy of it, then the first word on both copies would be the same. If I copied a photograph of myself, then the left ear on both copies would look the same.

In a proof, you often want to show that two line segments are the same length. If you can use theorems to show that two triangles of which these segments are part are congruent, then since every part of the two triangles is the same, these sides must be the same, too.

The trick is to make sure you choose *corresponding* parts! If you compared two pictures of me and claimed that the left ear of one had to be the same as the right ear of the other, you would be wrong. One ear may have been injured or have an earring in it, and the other not. You can only say they must be the same if they are both the same ear on identical pictures. The same is true with triangles. So when we talk about congruence, we have to name the triangles in the same order. These triangles are congruent:

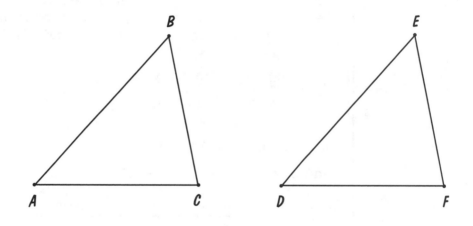

I have to say that *ABC* is congruent to *DEF* to show the order in which I am taking the triangles; then sides *AB* and *DE* are congruent, and so are *BC* and *EF*. I can't say that triangles *ABC* and *EFD* are congruent, because *AB* is not the same length as *EF*. But when I state clearly which parts correspond, then I can say that *AB* and *DE* are corresponding parts and therefore must be congruent. If they weren't, the triangles wouldn't be the same!

When do you use CPCTC? When you know that two triangles are congruent and want to say something about their angles or sides. Why? In order to prove congruence of angles or segments.

—*Dr. Math, The Math Forum*

Dear Dr. Math,

I have no idea whatsoever what I'm doing. It's so overwhelming that I can't even begin to try and figure it out. Please help me. I'll give you a sample problem:

Complete each of the following proofs.

(There's a figure of two triangles put together to make a slanty rectangle, and each corner of this slanty rectangle is a letter. The top left is G, the bottom left is T, the bottom right is A, and the top right is O.)

Alongside the figure is

Given: $GO \parallel TA$,
         $GT \parallel OA$

Show: $\triangle GOT \cong \triangle ATO$

Underneath the figure is

Statement	Reason
1. $GO \parallel TA$, $GT \parallel OA$	
2. $\angle GOT \cong \angle ATO$	
3. $OT \cong TO$	
4. $\angle GTO \cong \angle AOT$	
5. $\triangle GOT \cong \triangle ATO$	

Yours truly,
Qian

Hi, Qian,

A proof is just an orderly explanation of why you can be sure something is true. We take one step at a time and give a reason for everything we say so that there can be no doubt. In your problem, you are given the proof (the "statements"), and you just have to figure out why each step was done (filling in the "reasons"). Let's go through it together. First, I'll draw the diagram:

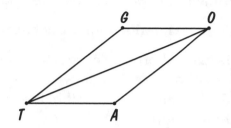

Now we'll take the statements one at a time:

1. $GO \parallel TA$, $GT \parallel OA$

This is easy: it's just what they gave us to start with, so we write our reason as

Given

2. $\angle GOT \cong \angle ATO$

Why should these two angles be congruent? Look at where they are in the figure:

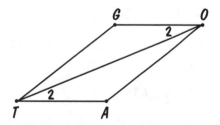

I've marked them with a 2; this should remind you of a diagram you have seen that looked like this:

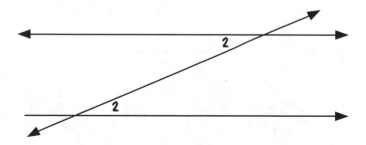

We have two parallel lines and a transversal; the angles 2 are called alternate interior angles. There's a theorem that alternate interior angles are congruent. There's our reason:

Alternate interior angles are congruent

This is just a short way of saying, "*TO* is a transversal of the parallel lines *GO* and *TA* (which we know to be parallel by statement 1), so by this theorem we know that the alternate interior angles *GOT* and *ATO* are congruent."

3. $OT \cong TO$

Here we have the opposite problem: this is so obvious we wonder why it was stated at all and why it will help us. It's here just so that a later statement can refer to it; all it's saying is that *OT* is equal to itself. The reason can be stated as something like

Reflexive property of equality

("Reflexive" means that the equal sign is like a mirror, and the image it "reflects" is the same as the original.) You probably have a list of names of obvious rules like this for filling in this sort of reason.

4. $\angle GTO \cong \angle AOT$

I'll let you work out what the reason for this is; it's essentially the same as step 2.

5. $\triangle GOT \cong \triangle ATO$

How can we prove that two triangles are congruent? You probably have several theorems along those lines; if we look at the two triangles and line them up so that the letters match, we can see what statements 2, 3, and 4 tell us about them:

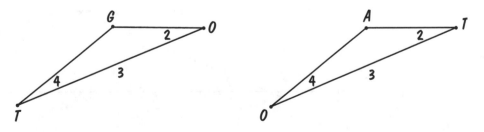

I've marked the facts in statements 2, 3, and 4 with their numbers. (You can see why the letters in each of those statements are in a specific order such as $OT \cong TO$; that makes them match up just right in this pair of triangles. Everything has been leading up to this.) Notice that we have two angles and the included side—ASA. Now we know why statement 3 was there! And the reason for this final statement is

ASA congruence theorem

We're done. Of course, we could actually go further; knowing that these triangles are congruent, we could prove that pairs of opposite sides of a parallelogram are congruent. But we were told to stop here, so we will.

I've included a lot of essential hints in what I've said, such as drawing the two triangles separately to help you see the parts in the proof, so take your time thinking through how I did this. And you'll be able to use the same methods in other proofs.

—*Dr. Math, The Math Forum*

esources on the Web

Learn more about triangles and congruence at these sites:

Math Forum: Geometry Problem of the Week: Another Ambiguous Angle?

mathforum.org/geopow/solutions/solution.ehtml?puzzle=15

Given isosceles triangle *ABC* with *BE* perpendicular to *AD*, if angle *ACB* is *x*, what is angle *CBE*?

Math Forum: Geometry Problem of the Week: Construct an Isosceles Triangle

mathforum.org/pow/solutio63.html

Find at least three different ways to construct an isosceles triangle (a construction is a set of steps that, when repeated over and over, will always yield the figure you want—in this case, an isosceles triangle).

Math Forum: Geometry Problem of the Week: The Folding Ruler

mathforum.org/geopow/solutions/solution.ehtml?puzzle=208

Describe all of the possible triangles that can be made with the full length of a 6-foot-long folding wooden ruler.

Math Forum: Geometry Problem of the Week: Making a Map

mathforum.org/geopow/solutions/solution.ehtml?puzzle=213

Given a list of relationships between five different objects, explain which ones you could uniquely place on a map.

Math Forum: Geometry Problem of the Week: Napoleon's River

mathforum.org/geopow/solutions/solution.ehtml?puzzle=106

A soldier uses the visor of his cap to measure the distance across a river.

Math Forum: Geometry Problem of the Week: The North Hunterdon Triangle

mathforum.org/geopow/solutions/solution.ehtml?puzzle=226

Given the coordinates of two points, find all possible locations of a third, such that the three would form an isosceles or equilateral triangle.

Math Forum: Geometry Problem of the Week: Scintillating Similarity

mathforum.org/geopow/solutions/solution.ehtml?puzzle=31

Given a triangle with sides of 3, 4, and 6, what is the perimeter of the smallest triangle that is similar to the first one and has one side with length 12?

Math Forum: Paper Folding Activity

mathforum.org/alejandre/escot/folding.html

Students fold a sheet of paper (a manipulative) and also simulate folding using a Java Sketchpad activity to observe geometric relations.

Shodor Organization: Project Interactivate: Triangle Explorer

shodor.org/interactivate/activities/triangle/index.html

Students study the nature of triangles and their areas.

PART 4 Quadrilaterals and Other Polygons

Polygons are figures made up of connected straight line segments. *Poly-* means "many," and *-gon* comes from the Greek word for "knee" (think of a knee as an angle). Triangles and quadrilaterals are two kinds of polygons. In this part, we'll look at some of the properties of polygons and their angles, review the seven kinds of quadrilaterals and their properties, and talk about how to find the area and perimeter of different quadrilaterals.

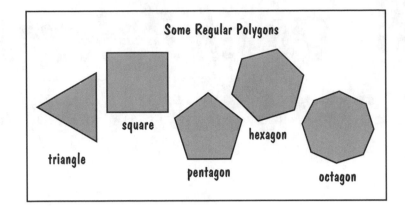

In this part, Dr. Math explains

- properties of polygons
- properties of quadrilaterals
- area and perimeter of quadrilaterals

Properties of Polygons

Many of the shapes in our world are polygons, such as soccer fields, road signs, floors, billiards tables, and computer screens. We can talk about their edge lengths, the measures of their angles, their areas, and their perimeters. Many properties apply to all polygons, but there are also specific things that we need to remember about particular ones.

Regular and Irregular Polygons

Dear Dr. Math,

What is the difference between a regular polygon and an equilateral polygon? I know that an equilateral triangle has three sides of equal length, and it is also a regular polygon. This is not true for polygons with more sides. Why?

Yours truly,

Qian

Hi, Qian,

The easiest demonstration is a rhombus. A rhombus is an equilateral polygon, but it is not necessarily regular. A regular polygon is a polygon where all the sides have equal length and all angles have equal measure. So a rhombus is equilateral but doesn't have to be regular. A square, which is a rhombus whose angles are all 90 degrees, is both equilateral *and* equiangular, so it's regular.

—*Dr. Math, The Math Forum*

<table>
<tr><td>

Interior Angle Sums of Polygons

</td><td>

Dear Dr. Math,

What can you conclude about the sum of the interior angles of a pentagon? A triangle? A quadrilateral? A hexagon?

   Does the sum depend on whether the polygon is convex? Why?

   What would you predict the sum of the interior angles of a twenty-sided polygon to be? How do you calculate this? Would the calculation be 20 · 360 because there are 360 degrees in a quadrilateral?

   Can you please help me?

Yours truly,

Quentin

</td></tr>
</table>

Hi, Quentin,

You had a good idea there to work from a simple case up to the big polygon. Unfortunately, your guess was off because you didn't see just how the smaller case relates to the big one.

   Let's look at the simplest cases first. For a triangle, there's an important theorem that tells you that the sum of the interior angles is 180 degrees. From this you can figure out the rest.

   Let's look at a rectangle next. Here you can see the answer in two ways. First, you know that all the angles of a rectangle are 90 degrees, and there are four of them, so the sum is 4 · 90 = 360 degrees.

Let's look at this another way. Draw a diagonal across the rectangle to divide it into two triangles:

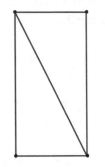

The sum of the interior angles of each triangle is 180 degrees, and all the interior angles of the triangle make up the interior angles of the rectangle. Since there are two triangles in the rectangle, the sum of the interior angles of the rectangle is 2 · 180 = 360 degrees.

This argument doesn't depend on having a rectangle. Any **convex** quadrilateral will do. (That's the kind with all interior angles measuring less than 180 degrees.)

Now see what you can do for a pentagon. Again you can start at one vertex and draw two diagonals. This divides the pentagon into three triangles, and you can see that the sum of the angles of the pentagon is 3 · 180 = 540 degrees.

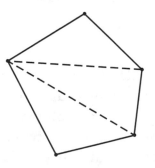

Now we should begin to see a pattern. Let's make a table:

Number of Sides	Sum of Interior Angles
3	$1 \cdot 180$
4	$2 \cdot 180$
5	$3 \cdot 180$
. . .	. . .
20	?

This even works with **concave polygons**—those having at least one interior angle measuring greater than 180 degrees. The idea is that no matter how the polygon twists and turns, you can always cut off a triangle that stays entirely inside the polygon, so what is left is a polygon with one fewer side.

As in a lot of math problems, the general idea is to start with the simplest cases, where you can see what is happening, and work your way up to more complicated cases, looking for a general pattern.

—*Dr. Math, The Math Forum*

REGULAR POLYGON ANGLE MEASURES

Notice that once you have the sum of the interior angles of
any regular polygon, you can divide by the number of
vertices in that polygon to get the angle
measure of each interior angle.
Here's a heptagon, for example:

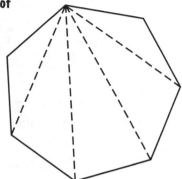

We can divide it internally into five triangles, so its angle sum must be 5 · 180,
or 900 degrees. Divide that by 7, the total number of vertices, and you get about
128.57 degrees, the angle measure of a regular heptagon.

Exterior Angles in a Polygon

Dear Dr. Math,

Is there a theorem for concave polygons
about the sum of the interior and the sum
of the exterior angles?

I know that for convex polygons the sum
of the interior angles is $(n - 2)180$ and
the sum of the exterior angles is 360. However, my geometry class believes that we
might have proven that for concave polygons
the sum of the interior angles is still
$(n - 2)180$, but the sum of the exterior
angles is 540. Do you know if this can be
found in any textbook or if it has been
proven before?

Yours truly,

Qian

Hi, Qian,

The theorem you refer to about the exterior angles of a convex polygon applies to concave polygons as well, *if* you take the direction of the exterior angles into account. If you don't, then you may get a variety of sums, depending on how many angles turn in each direction. Take this example, a concave hexagon with two "dents":

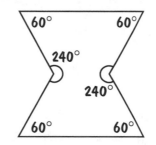

The sum of the interior angles is 60 + 60 + 240 + 60 + 60 + 240 = 720 = (6 – 2)180 as expected.

Exterior angles work a little bit differently. Instead of measuring the whole angle, you extend one of the sides of the polygon and measure the angle between that extension and the side of the polygon. For example, the exterior angle of a square is 90 degrees, not 270 degrees. You then continue around the polygon in the same direction, extending each side in a similar fashion.

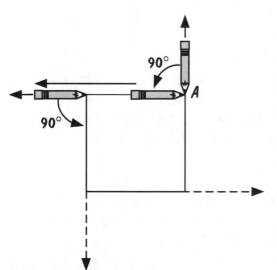

Imagine using your pencil to keep track of the number of degrees. If we are working with a square, start with the end of the pencil at point *A*, running along one side of the square extended. Rotate it 90 degrees, then slide it to the next vertex. Rotate again and slide. Keep going until the pencil returns to its starting point. You'll see that the pencil has turned 360 degrees.

If the figure is convex, we'll do exactly the same thing. What you'll notice is that for some of the turns, you'll turn *back* some number of degrees.

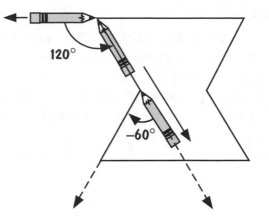

First, the pencil turns 120 degrees. Then it slides to the next vertex and turns 60 degrees but in the other direction. These count as "negative" degrees. Again, if we go all the way around the figure in this manner, we'll see that the pencil has turned a total of 360 degrees. This is always 360, because in going around a polygon you always make one complete turn, and the sum of the exterior angles in this sense tells how far you have turned. It is this sum that can be used to prove the sum of the interior angles, since each interior angle is the supplement of its exterior angle. Where A is each interior angle, B is each exterior angle, and n is the number of angles:

sum of A = sum of $(180 - B) = 180n -$ sum of $B =$
$180n - 360 = (n - 2)180$

In our example, the supplement of interior angle $A = 240$ is $B = 180 - 240 = -60$. That's not how we normally think of supplements, but it's the only way that makes sense for reflex angles like this.

Now, if we sum the absolute values of the exterior angles, not treating them as signed angles, we get a different answer:

$120 + 120 + 60 + 120 + 120 + 60 = 600$

You might like to play with this and see whether you can get any sum at all by changing the number and size of the negative angles, or if there is some restriction on possible sums.

—*Dr. Math, The Math Forum*

Interior Angles Not 360 Degrees

Dear Dr. Math,

I have calculated that the value of an angle in a quadrilateral is 65 degrees. The other angles are 12, 104, and 27 degrees, and the sum is equal to 208, not 360. Is this correct?

Yours truly,

Quentin

Hi, Quentin,

I suspect that you have a nonconvex quadrilateral, and one of your angles is not an interior angle. It's the interior angles that add up to 360 degrees.

In particular, if the shape looks something like

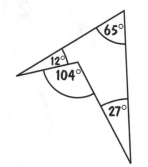

then the interior angle corresponding to 104 degrees is 360 − 104 = 256, and the sum of interior angles is 12 + 256 + 27 + 65 = 360 as expected.

—*Dr. Math, The Math Forum*

Properties of Quadrilaterals

Polygons with only four sides are called "quadrilaterals." There are seven different types of quadrilaterals, ranging from the very general scalene quadrilateral to the very constrained square.

The Seven Quadrilaterals

Dear Dr. Math,

I really need to know the seven types of quadrilaterals. Please give me a hand!

Yours truly,

Qian

Dear Qian,

I think you're talking about these:

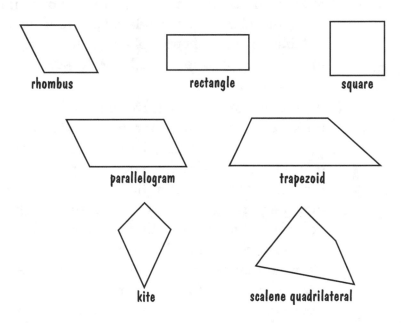

Here are some things to note:

1. A **rhombus** is an equilateral quadrilateral (all sides have the same length).

2. A **rectangle** is an equiangular quadrilateral (all angles have the same measure).

3. A **square** is an equilateral, equiangular quadrilateral, or simply a regular quadrilateral. Every square is also a rhombus (because it's equilateral) and a rectangle (because it's equiangular).

4. A **parallelogram** is any quadrilateral with exactly two pairs of parallel sides. Every rhombus is a parallelogram and so is every rectangle. And if every rectangle is, then so is every square. And if every rhombus is, then so is every square.

5. There are two definitions in common use for **trapezoid**. The traditional American definition is a quadrilateral with *exactly*

one pair of parallel sides. The British and "new" American definition is a quadrilateral with *at least* one pair of parallel sides. In this book we will use the second definition. This means any parallelogram (including a rhombus, a rectangle, or a square) may be considered a trapezoid, because each has at least one pair of parallel sides. (If the trapezoid is isosceles, then the nonparallel sides have the same length *and* the base angles are equal.)

6. A **kite** may or may not have parallel sides; what it does have for sure are two pairs of adjacent sides with equal lengths. That is, instead of being across from each other, the sides with equal lengths are next to each other. So a kite can look like the kind of toy you'd fly in a field on a windy day. But a rhombus and a square are also special cases of a kite: they have two pairs of adjacent sides that have equal length, but the equal lengths are also equal to each other.

   Just as there are two definitions in use for the trapezoid, there are two definitions for the kite. We use the one given above; some people use one that says the two pairs of congruent sides must have different lengths, so for them, a rhombus (and therefore a square) is not a kite.

7. A **scalene quadrilateral** has four unequal sides that are not parallel.

Knowing these facts about the different quadrilaterals, we can draw the following diagram, which shows us how the quadrilaterals are related:

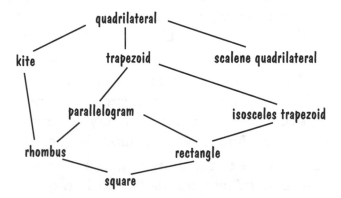

Each quadrilateral has the properties of the ones above and connected to it in the tree. So, for example, the diagonals of an isosceles trapezoid are congruent. Since the rectangle is an isosceles trapezoid, its diagonals are also congruent. The kite has diagonals that are perpendicular, and the parallelogram has diagonals that bisect each other. Since the rhombus is a kite and a parallelogram, its diagonals are perpendicular *and* bisect each other. So the square, which is both a rectangle and a rhombus, has diagonals that are congruent perpendicular bisectors!

There are many problems that use the properties of quadrilaterals and the relationships between them. If you try to keep in mind the ways in which the quadrilaterals are related, you won't have to remember everything about every individual quadrilateral.

—Dr. Math, The Math Forum

Angles of a Parallelogram

Dear Dr. Math,

In parallelogram *ABCD*, ∠*ABC* = 2 · ∠*BCD*. What is the measure of ∠*ADC*?

Yours truly,

Quentin

Hi, Quentin,

You must remember that adjacent angles in a parallelogram are supplementary—that is, they add up to 180 degrees. So your problem becomes one of algebra.

If the measure of ∠*BCD* is x, then the measure of ∠*ABC* must be $2x$.

Then we know that $2x + x = 180$, so $x = 60$ degrees. ∠*ADC* must have a measure of 120 degrees.

—Dr. Math, The Math Forum

Dear Dr. Math,

The lengths of the diagonals of a parallelogram are 10 and 24. If the length of one side of the parallelogram is 13, what is the perimeter of the parallelogram?

Is this right? Two sides are 13. The other two sides are 10.9. I used $a^2 + b^2 = c^2$:

$a^2 + (5)^2 = (12)^2$

$a^2 + 25 = 144$

$a^2 = 144 - 25$

$a^2 = 119$

$a = 10.9$

$13 + 13 + 10.9 + 10.9 = 47.8$

Yours truly,

Qian

Hi, Qian,

You've made a nice try at solving this problem. However, your analysis is not quite correct. Let me try to explain why and how you might want to think about this problem.

First of all, you are correct in recognizing that the diagonals of a parallelogram bisect each other. Consequently, the segments of each diagonal are 5 and 12. You know that one side of this parallelogram is 13. Therefore, one of the inner triangles has sides of 5, 12, and 13. Is this a right triangle? If so, which side is the hypotenuse?

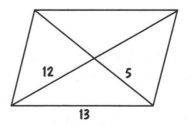

You should remember that in a right triangle the longest side is always the hypotenuse. So if this triangle is a right triangle, 13 must be the hypotenuse. Therefore, the legs, a and b, are 5 and 12.

You must first show that this triangle is a right triangle. To do this, see if $a^2 + b^2$ is equal to 13^2.

$$c^2 = 5^2 + 12^2$$

$$c^2 = 25 + 144$$

$$c = \sqrt{169} = 13$$

Therefore, the triangle is indeed a right triangle, since $a^2 + b^2 = c^2$.

Since the triangle is right, then the angle opposite the 13-side is a right angle. Therefore, the diagonals are perpendicular to each other, and all the inner triangles are right triangles with sides of 5, 12, and 13.

Since the hypotenuses of each triangle are equal to the same number, they are equal to each other, and since each hypotenuse is also a side of the parallelogram, then by definition the parallelogram is a rhombus. Its perimeter is $4 \cdot 13 = 52$.

The secret to solving this problem correctly then is to first show that a right triangle exists by using the converse of the Pythagorean theorem and showing that $a^2 + b^2 = c^2$. Second, show that the parallelogram has four equal sides (and is a rhombus).

This was a tricky problem. You had the right ideas but made a few wrong turns. Hope that this explanation is helpful.

—*Dr. Math, The Math Forum*

Proving Diagonals Perpendicular	Dear Dr. Math,
	Given the points $A(-4,1)$, $B(2,3)$, $C(4,9)$, and $D(-2,7)$, show that quadrilateral $ABCD$ is a parallelogram with perpendicular diagonals.
	Yours truly,
	Quentin

Hi, Quentin,

I'm going to draw a rough diagram of the four points so that I can see what we're talking about.

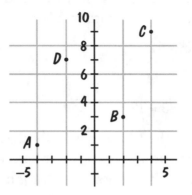

Let's show that the two diagonals of the quadrilateral are perpendicular—that is, if we drew a line passing through A and C and another line passing through B and D, those two lines would be perpendicular to each other.

How can you tell if two lines are perpendicular? One way, which you'll most likely want to use here, is to look at their slopes. If the product of the slopes of two lines is equal to -1, then the two lines are perpendicular. So let's find the slopes of the two diagonals.

$$\text{slope } AC = \frac{\text{rise}}{\text{run}}$$

$$= \frac{9-1}{4-(-4)}$$

$$= \frac{8}{8}$$

$$= 1$$

Similarly (you'll want to work this out for yourself), the slope of line BD is -1. If we take the two slopes and multiply them, we get

$$\text{slope } AC \cdot \text{slope } BD = 1 \cdot -1 = -1$$

and since the product is –1, we know that these two lines are perpendicular. Does this make sense?

We're also asked to show that the figure is a parallelogram, so let's see if one pair of opposite sides is parallel. We'll compare the slopes of DC and AB.

$$\text{slope } DC = \frac{\text{rise}}{\text{run}} = \frac{7-9}{-2-4} = \frac{-2}{-6} = \frac{1}{3}$$

$$\text{slope } AB = \frac{\text{rise}}{\text{run}} = \frac{1-3}{-4-2} = \frac{-2}{-6} = \frac{1}{3}$$

Since those slopes are equal, the sides are parallel.

We can do the same with the other pair of sides, and we'll find that they're also parallel. So this is indeed a parallelogram with perpendicular diagonals. (The problem didn't ask you this, but we can actually say that the figure is a rhombus, since a rhombus is a parallelogram with perpendicular diagonals.)

—Dr. Math, The Math Forum

Is This a Square?

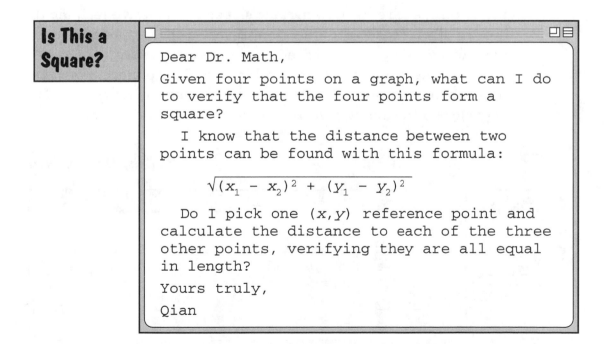

Dear Dr. Math,

Given four points on a graph, what can I do to verify that the four points form a square?

I know that the distance between two points can be found with this formula:

$$\sqrt{(x_1 - x_2)^2 + (y_1 - y_2)^2}$$

Do I pick one (x, y) reference point and calculate the distance to each of the three other points, verifying they are all equal in length?

Yours truly,

Qian

Hi, Qian,

No. If you did so, you'd be comparing two sides of the quadrilateral and one diagonal.

We can use the properties of a square to figure this out. One method would be to find the length of each side (the distance between two adjacent vertices) and show that all four sides are equal. You must also show that each side is perpendicular to the two adjacent sides. This is true if the product of the slopes of the two lines is –1. (See the previous answer on page 104 for an explanation of how to calculate this.)

You don't have to do every one of these calculations. For instance, once you've shown that the four sides are of equal length, it's enough to show that a single pair of adjacent sides is perpendicular. A rhombus with one right angle is a square.

Another method would be to show that the diagonals are congruent, perpendicular, and bisect each other, since that means the figure must be a square (diagonals can be really useful!). To show that they're congruent, you can find the length of each one using the distance formula. To show that they're perpendicular, you can find the slope of each and show that the slopes are negative reciprocals of each other. Then to show that they bisect each other, find the midpoint of each diagonal and see if they're the same point.

There are many other ways to do this. But before jumping in, think about what you know is true of squares and what you need to know to confirm that a quadrilateral is a square and not some other quadrilateral.

—Dr. Math, The Math Forum

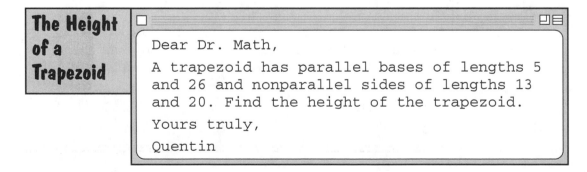

The Height of a Trapezoid

Dear Dr. Math,

A trapezoid has parallel bases of lengths 5 and 26 and nonparallel sides of lengths 13 and 20. Find the height of the trapezoid.

Yours truly,

Quentin

Hi, Quentin,

Look at the trapezoid below.

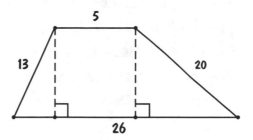

I've drawn in a rectangle that I want to cut out of the trapezoid. I'll glue the remaining triangles together; that will leave me with a triangle whose sides I know:

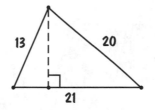

There are several ways to work out the altitude of this triangle. Here's one way. I can relabel the bottom of the triangle as x and $21 - x$ and label the height as h.

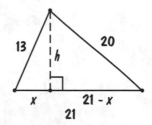

We have two right triangles, so we can use the Pythagorean theorem to solve each for the height.

$$h^2 + x^2 = 13^2 \qquad\qquad (21 - x)^2 + h^2 = 20^2$$
$$h^2 = 13^2 - x^2 \qquad\qquad h^2 = 20^2 - (21 - x)^2$$

We don't actually have to find h, but we can stop right now and notice that our two statements are equal to h^2, so they must be equal to each other. So we get the following equation, which we could solve for x:

$$13^2 - x^2 = 20^2 - (21 - x)^2$$
$$169 - x^2 = 400 - [(21 - x)(21 - x)]$$
$$169 - x^2 = 400 - [441 - 42x + x^2]$$
$$169 - x^2 = 400 - 441 + 42x - x^2$$
$$169 = -41 + 42x$$
$$210 = 42x$$
$$x = 5$$

We then use x to find h.

—*Dr. Math, The Math Forum*

Right. I'm getting $h^2 = 144$, so $h = 12$. Does that sound right to you?

Ah, we can use the Pythagorean theorem on the little triangle. It's height is the unknown, and it's a leg, so $5^2 + h^2 = 13^2$.

Dear Dr. Math,

I have to prove that the legs of a trapezoid are congruent if the diagonals of the trapezoid are congruent.

I started by stating the bases are parallel to each other and I got the alternate interior angles congruent. Then I drew a parallel line to one of the diagonals because of the parallel postulate. That was as far as I could get. I don't understand what else to do. Please help.

Yours truly,

Qian

Hi, Qian,

Let's consider the following trapezoid:

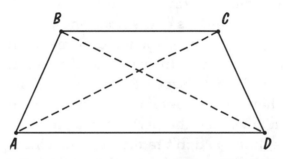

I would look for a pair of congruent triangles with which we can prove the final result. If the bases are *AD* and *BC*, then, for example, triangles *ABD* and *DCA* look as if they should be congruent, and these include the diagonals. There's another pair of corresponding sides, but I don't immediately see that the included angles have to be congruent. How can we show that angles *ADB* and *DAC* are congruent?

One way I see is to draw the altitudes from *B* and *C* to side *AD*. Since *AD* and *BC* are parallel, those are equal. Can you see a way to use this fact to prove that the angles are congruent?

What I did here was to work backward: the last steps will involve proving two triangles congruent. What do I need to do this, and how can I get there? Another thing that led me to this idea was imagining what it would take to construct a trapezoid with congruent diagonals. I might start with parallel lines on which the bases have to lie and two equal sticks for the diagonals. When I saw that in order to go from one line to the other they would have to be at the same angle (and why), that gave me the idea I needed.

This is how proofs are generally found: working from both ends and playing with the materials we have in order to see what we can do with them. It's fun that way, too!

—Dr. Math, The Math Forum

Area and Perimeter of Quadrilaterals

The **perimeter** of any shape is simply the distance around the shape. Add up the lengths of the sides and you've found the perimeter. The prefix *peri-* means "around," and *-meter* means "to measure." There are formulas you can use to find the perimeter of specific quadrilaterals and other shapes. For example, if the edge length of a square is s, then the perimeter is $4s$. If the length of a rectangle is l and the width is w, then the perimeter is just $2l + 2w$. You could memorize those, but you don't really need to, since you could come up with them when you need them if you understand the concept. Perimeter is measured in "linear" units, such as inches, meters, or miles.

The **area** of a shape could be thought of as the amount of paint you'd need to paint it or the amount of material you would need to cover it. The formula for the area of a rectangle is length multiplied by width. As you'll see below, all of the formulas for the areas of quadrilaterals are related in some way, and if you can remember those relations, you don't really need to memorize all of the separate formulas. Area is measured in "square" units, such as square centimeters, square yards, or square kilometers.

The Perimeter of a Rectangle

Dear Dr. Math,

I need an equation for this problem: the length of a rectangle is 9 inches more than half the width. Find the length if the perimeter is 60 inches.

Yours truly,

Quentin

Hi, Quentin,

Let x be the width of the rectangle. Half the width is $\frac{x}{2}$. Then the length is 9 inches more than (+9) half the width ($\frac{x}{2}$), or $\frac{x}{2}$ + 9. The perimeter would be 2 widths plus 2 lengths or

$$P = 2(x) + 2\left(\frac{x}{2} + 9\right) = 60$$

—Dr. Math, The Math Forum

Finding the Perimeter and Area

Dear Dr. Math,

I'm a little confused about perimeter and area. I use addition to find the perimeter, and I use multiplication to find the area just the way my teacher taught me. I can do rectangles and squares but not trapezoids, triangles, and other funny-looking shapes. We had to do this problem with a parallelogram that was 27 yards across at the top and bottom, 13 yards at the sides, and 12 yards in the parallelogram. I came up with 240 yards for the area, but the answer was really 324 yards. Can you help?

Yours truly,

Qian

Hi, Qian,

Perimeter isn't that hard if you remember that it is always the sum of the lengths of all the sides of the figure. Area is harder because you have a different formula for each kind of figure. You need to be careful to use the right formula for the figure and to know the meaning of each quantity in the formula.

Let's look at a diagram of your parallelogram. I assume that when you say "12 yards in the parallelogram" you mean the height—the length of a line joining the top and bottom and perpendicular to both of them.

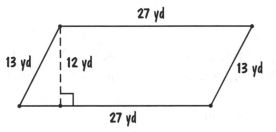

In your example of the parallelogram, the first mistake you made is to use the formula for a trapezoid. This formula is

$$\text{area of trapezoid} = \frac{(\text{top} + \text{bottom})}{2} \cdot \text{height}$$

You must be sure that top and bottom are the lengths of the parallel sides. You can actually use this formula for a parallelogram, because a parallelogram is a special kind of trapezoid with the top and bottom of the same length. However, instead of using the top and bottom in the formula, you used the length and width.

It's probably easier to use the formula for a parallelogram, which is

$$\text{area of parallelogram} = \text{base} \cdot \text{height}$$

This formula works for rectangles and squares, too, because they are special kinds of parallelograms. But you must be careful not to confuse the length of a side with the height. These are the same for a rectangle or a square but not for most parallelograms.

The height measures the distance between the base of the figure and its highest point. So in this case, the base is 27 yards and the height is 12 yards. Then using the formula,

$$\text{area of parallelogram} = \text{base} \cdot \text{height}$$
$$= 27 \text{ yd} \cdot 12 \text{ yd}$$
$$= 324 \text{ yd}^2$$

(Don't forget that area is measured in square units, like square yards [yd^2], not just yards!)

So once again, these are the three main things to remember:

1. Use the right formula for the figure—know the definitions of parallelogram, trapezoid, and so on.

2. Know the definitions of the terms used in the formulas (base, height, and so on) so that you can use the right number for each.

3. Don't be confused when a figure has more numbers than you need! You didn't need the length of the side to figure out the area; it is only needed for the perimeter.

—*Dr. Math, The Math Forum*

How to Remember Area Formulas

Dear Dr. Math,

I was wondering if there was a good way to help me memorize the formulas for areas of different shapes. I am having a lot of trouble doing that and I need help. Is there a funny saying or something?

Yours truly,

Quentin

Hi, Quentin,

I remember when I was learning to read music that someone taught me "Every Good Boy Does Fine" or something like that, but I don't even remember what it's for! I don't know of any funny saying or anything that can help you remember area formulas. But I think there is a better way to remember them.

First, there are two things you have to memorize. Only two, though!

1. The area of a rectangle is width · length.

2. The area of a circle is π · radius · radius.

Then, if you don't remember the formula for other area problems, you can use those two facts to figure out the area. A square is easy enough to figure out. It is just a special type of rectangle in which width = length. So you just multiply side · side and you've got it.

For another example, you can find the area of a triangle using the formula for the area of a rectangle:

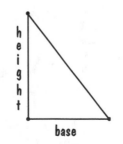

The area is $\frac{1}{2}$ · base · height. How do I remember that? Well, I imagine this rectangle:

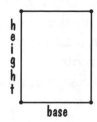

and I remember that the area will be base · height. Then I look at my triangle again with an imaginary rectangle drawn around it:

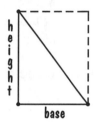

The diagonal line cuts the rectangle in half. That means the area of the triangle is half the area of the rectangle.

What about this triangle?

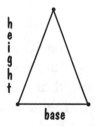

Here I imagine another rectangle around it like this:

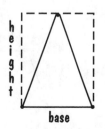

Again, the area of the rectangle is base · height. To convince yourself that the area of the triangle is half of that, draw the figure above on a piece of paper and cut out the rectangle. Then cut the triangle out and save the two scrap pieces. If you put the two scrap pieces next to each other, they will make a triangle that's the same size as the first triangle.

What about other strange shapes? Here's a fun one, the parallelogram:

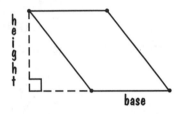

To do this one, imagine a rectangle like this:

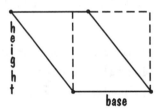

The area of that rectangle is again base · height. If you draw it and cut it out, you will see that the little area on the left that was not included in the imaginary rectangle is exactly the same size as the little area on the right that we added to the imaginary rectangle. So the parallelogram's area is also base · height (notice the difference here between base · height and side · side).

Here's one of the trickiest, the trapezoid:

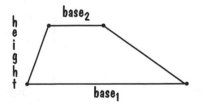

Imagine a rectangle like this:

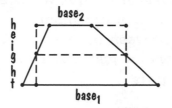

Just like with the parallelogram, the area we left out on the bottom is equal in size to the area we added on the top. That means the area of the trapezoid is the same size as the area of the rectangle we're imagining.

So far so good, but what is the area of the rectangle? Here's where trapezoids get a little bit tricky: the height of the imaginary rectangle is the same as the height of the trapezoid. But the base is smaller than base$_1$ and bigger than base$_2$. How big is it?

Let's look at the figure again:

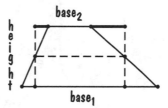

The thicker line segments mark the part of the base that we added to base$_2$. So the base of our imaginary rectangle is base$_2$ plus the length of the thick line segments.

So how long is that? Look at this figure:

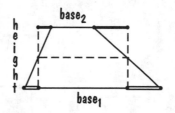

The hollow line segments represent the part of the base that we cut out of base$_1$. So the base of our imaginary rectangle is base$_1$—the length of the hollow line segment.

Here's the crucial point: the length that we cut off of base$_1$ is *exactly equal* to the length we added to base$_2$.

So the base of the imaginary rectangle equals some number that is halfway between base$_1$ and base$_2$. How do you find a number halfway between? Just take the average. So the base of our imaginary rectangle is

$$\frac{base_2 + base_1}{2}$$

So the area of our imaginary rectangle is

$$height \cdot \frac{base_2 + base_1}{2}$$

And since the imaginary rectangle is the same size as the real trapezoid, that must be the area of the trapezoid.

Of course, on a test you won't be able to go through *all* of that from scratch. So you should practice making imaginary rectangles from the figures you're given until you can do it quickly, then you should be able to go through any area problem without much trouble.

Plus, if you learn the reasons why areas equal what they do instead of learning a funny rhyme, then if you ever forget the formulas completely, you can always figure them out again; but if you ever forgot a rhyme, you'd be stuck with nowhere to go. Learning math takes a lot of practice, but if you try to learn why things are the way they are instead of just memorizing formulas with no reason behind them, you'll do better and you'll enjoy it more.

There are a lot more types of figures in geometry than I just told you about. Here's my last bit of advice: whenever you come to a new figure and you want to learn the area or volume or whatever, try to imagine a simpler figure drawn around it and try to understand how the size of the new figure is different from the simple one you imagined. That way you can understand the area of new figures without having to memorize more stuff. And if you ever come across a figure you don't get, just write back and I'll try to help you understand it.

If there are other postulates and theorems that you're stuck on, try to understand why they are true, which should help you learn them. Feel free to write back if you have other questions about those as well.

—*Dr. Math, The Math Forum*

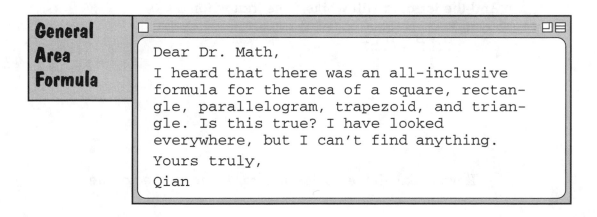

General Area Formula

Dear Dr. Math,

I heard that there was an all-inclusive formula for the area of a square, rectangle, parallelogram, trapezoid, and triangle. Is this true? I have looked everywhere, but I can't find anything.

Yours truly,

Qian

Hi, Qian,

Let's start with the most complicated (that is, least symmetric) shape, which is a trapezoid:

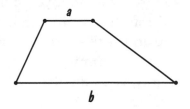

$$\text{area} = \text{height} \cdot \frac{a + b}{2}$$

In the case where a and b are equal, we have a parallelogram:

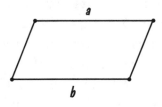

$$\text{area} = \text{height} \cdot \frac{a + b}{2}$$

And the formula still works. Note that when $a = b$,

$$\frac{a + b}{2} = \frac{b + b}{2}$$

$$= \frac{2 \cdot b}{2}$$

$$= b$$

If we make all the angles square, we have a rectangle:

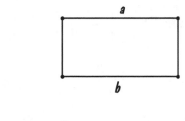

$$\text{area} = \text{height} \cdot \frac{a + b}{2}$$

And the formula still works. If we make the width the same as the height, we have a square:

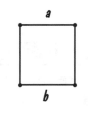

$$\text{area} = \text{height} \cdot \frac{a + b}{2}$$

And the formula still works! The principal difference is that when you have a rectangle or a square, the height is easy to find, whereas when you have a trapezoid or a parallelogram, the process can be somewhat more involved.

So what about a triangle? Well, if we draw the triangle so that the base is horizontal, then the value of the top base a is zero, so the formula gives us

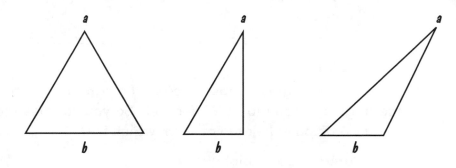

$$\text{area} = \text{height} \cdot \frac{a + b}{2}$$

$$= \text{height} \cdot \frac{0 + b}{2}$$

$$= \frac{1}{2} \cdot \text{height} \cdot b$$

So it works for a triangle, too—if you're willing to define a triangle as a quadrilateral with one zero-length side.

I hope this helps. Thanks for an interesting question!

—*Dr. Math, The Math Forum*

Rectangle to Parallelogram

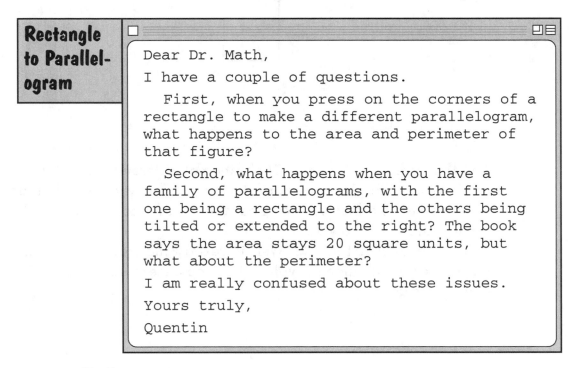

Dear Dr. Math,

I have a couple of questions.

First, when you press on the corners of a rectangle to make a different parallelogram, what happens to the area and perimeter of that figure?

Second, what happens when you have a family of parallelograms, with the first one being a rectangle and the others being tilted or extended to the right? The book says the area stays 20 square units, but what about the perimeter?

I am really confused about these issues.

Yours truly,

Quentin

Hi, Quentin,

In fact, a rectangle is a special case of a parallelogram in which all the angles happen to be 90 degrees. So you can use the same formula to compute the area of each, which is

$$\text{area} = \text{base} \cdot \text{height}$$

As you squish a rectangle into a parallelogram, the sides don't change length, so the perimeter (which is just the sum of the lengths of the sides) must stay the same; but the height decreases, so the area must decrease, too.

If you have a set of parallelograms with the same side lengths, the rectangle will be the one with the largest area. The areas of the others can get as close to zero as you want by making two of the angles very close to zero and the other two angles very close to 180 degrees.

To see why this works, cut off the flaps at the ends of a cereal box. Look through the box to see a rectangle. Now start squishing the box by making it as flat as possible. The perimeter stays the same (since none of the sides are changing length), but the area decreases, like this:

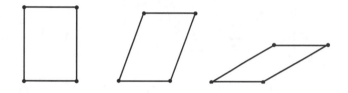

These all have the same perimeter but different areas.

I'm not entirely sure what your book is talking about—I suspect there are illustrations, which I would need to see—but it sounds to me as though the other possibility is that the base and height stay the same, like this:

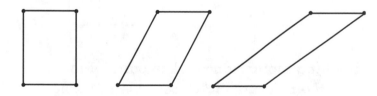

These all have the same area but different perimeters.

From your initial statement, it sounds as though you may be confused about the basic ideas of perimeter and area. If that's the case, you should probably take a look at our first book on geometry, *Dr. Math Introduces Geometry*.

—*Dr. Math, The Math Forum*

Dear Dr. Math,

Given: a quadrilateral where the midpoints of each side are connected to form a new quadrilateral inside the first. What is the ratio of the area of the larger quadrilateral to the smaller one?

I know that the ratio is 2:1; I solved it by drawing the quadrilateral as a square, and from there the problem was easy. However, I want to know if there is a way to solve this problem without drawing the quadrilateral as a square.

Yours truly,

Qian

Hi, Qian,

Let us consider a quadrilateral as you described it:

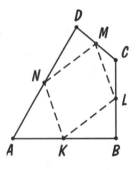

Note that, for instance, *KL* is parallel to and half the measure of *AC*, because in triangle *ABC*, segment *KL* is a midsegment. The same can be said about *MN*. So *MN* and *KL* are parallel and congruent. This tells us that *KLMN* is a parallelogram. Now let *X* and *Y* be the intersections of *AC* with *KN* and *LM*, respectively. And let *E* be the intersection of the altitude from *B* to *AC*.

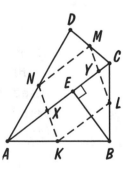

KLYX is a parallelogram, too. When KL is taken as the base, then the measure of the height of this parallelogram is half BE. We find

$$\text{area } KLYX = KL \cdot 0.5 \cdot BE$$
$$= 0.5 \cdot AC \cdot 0.5 \cdot BE$$
$$= 0.5 \cdot (0.5 \cdot AC \cdot BE)$$
$$= 0.5 \cdot \text{area } ABC$$

In the same way, we find that area $XYMN = 0.5 \cdot$ area ACD. Combining these two we find the desired result that

$$\text{area } KLMN = 0.5 \cdot \text{area } ABCD.$$

—Dr. Math, The Math Forum

Finding the Area of an Irregular Polygon Given the Length of Its Sides

Dear Dr. Math,

I am trying to determine the square footage of a piece of property. The problem is that it is not rectangular. The dimensions of the four sides in a clockwise order from the top are 43.61 feet, 133.64 feet, 146.96 feet, and 110.85 feet. I have tried dividing it into three parts (two right triangles and a rectangle) and have tried several different formulas I found on the Ask Dr. Math Web site, but it seems I don't have enough information without knowing at least one of the angles.

Yours truly,

Quentin

Hi, Quentin,

You're right—you can't determine the area of a quadrilateral from the lengths of the sides alone. Imagine that you have rods of the lengths above that are attached at their tips by pivoting joints. It should be clear that the whole thing can flex in such a way that wildly different shapes can be formed. If you have the length of either diagonal or any of the angles and you know it's concave or convex, you can work it out. With just the sides, you're out of luck.

For example, let's look at quadrilaterals with sides of 2, 3, 4, and 6. Here are a few examples:

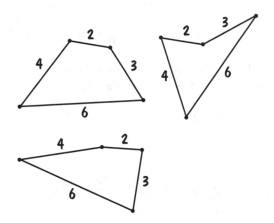

As you can see, even if we know the order of the sides, we can't determine what shape the quadrilateral must have. While three sides *do* determine a unique triangle, the same isn't true for quadrilaterals!

But let's say that we're told one of the diagonals is 4 (and we're told which diagonal). Now we've got only one choice:

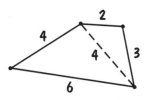

There are a variety of methods we can use to find the area of the two resulting triangles. The method I would probably choose in this situation, where we know the three sides, is Heron's formula, which works like this. If we are given a triangle with sides a, b, and c, then Heron's formula says that the

$$\text{area of the triangle} = \sqrt{s(s-a)(s-b)(s-c)}$$

where s is equal to half of the perimeter of the triangle: $\dfrac{a + b + c}{2}$.

In this case, the perimeter is 2 + 3 + 4 + 6 = 15, so half of that is $\frac{15}{2}$. What's under the square root sign works out to be $\frac{15}{2} \cdot \frac{11}{2} \cdot \frac{9}{2} \cdot \frac{7}{2}$. If you multiply that out, what do you get? You get $\frac{10{,}395}{16}$, or about 650. The square root of that is about 25.5, and that's the area of the smaller part of your shape. Now see if you can figure out the other part.

—Dr. Math, The Math Forum

Resources on the Web

Learn more about quadrilaterals and other polygons at these Math Forum sites:

Geometry Problem of the Week: The Coordinated Quadrilateral

mathforum.org/geopow/solutions/solution.ehtml?puzzle=134

A quadrilateral has vertices at (–3,6), (–1,–2), (7,–4), and (5,4). What kind of quadrilateral is it?

Geometry Problem of the Week: The Mystery Polygon

mathforum.org/geopow/archive/022897.geopow.html

I have a quadrilateral that has one pair of opposite sides congruent, the other pair not congruent, and a pair of opposite angles that are supplementary. What is this figure?

Geometry Problem of the Week: The Puzzling Parallelogram

mathforum.org/geopow/solutions/solution.ehtml?puzzle=61

Draw a parallelogram $ABCD$ with $AB = 10$. Draw EF with E between A and B and F between C and D such that EF divides the area of $ABCD$ in half. If $EF = 4$, what is FD?

Geometry Problem of the Week: Splitting a Hexagon

mathforum.org/geopow/archive/solutio88.html

Split a regular hexagon into three identical parts. What shape is each part? Split a regular hexagon into six identical parts at least two different ways. What shapes are your pieces? Split a regular hexagon into six identical kites.

Geometry Problem of the Week: Areas of Overlapping Squares

mathforum.org/geopow/solutions/19980313.geopow.html

Two congruent 10-inch by 10-inch squares overlap. A vertex of one square is at the center of the other square. What is the largest possible value for the area where they overlap?

Geometry Problem of the Week: Trapezoidal Garden

mathforum.org/geopow/solutions/19980410.geopow.html

Given trapezoid $ABCD$ with E on AD, F on BC, and EF parallel to AB, if AE is three-fourths of ED and BC is 14 feet, how long is FC?

Circles and Their Parts

Understanding and being able to use properties of circles and their parts is important in such areas as construction, operating satellites, cellular phone networks, and even search-and-rescue procedures! In this part, we'll look at the properties of circles and the objects related to them.

To make sure we're talking about the same things, let's look at an illustration and define the different terms and objects that we'll use in this section.

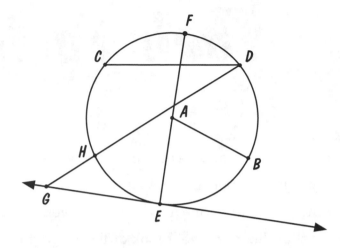

AB is a **radius**. It connects the center of the circle and a point on the circle.

CD is a **chord**. It connects two points on the circle.

EF is a **diameter**. It's a chord that passes through the center of the circle.

EG is a **tangent**. It intersects the circle at exactly one point and is perpendicular to *AE*.

GD is a **secant**. It intersects the circle at exactly two points.

∠*BAF* is a **central angle**. Its vertex is the center of the circle.

∠*CDH* is an **inscribed angle**. Its vertex is on the circle.

The curve of the circle between *B* and *E* is an arc. It's a minor arc because its degree measure is less than 180. Major arcs cover more than half the circle, measuring more than 180 degrees. An arc measuring exactly 180 degrees, whose endpoints are the endpoints of a diameter, is a semicircle.

Now we can talk about the properties of these objects and how we can use them to solve problems and find other measurements.

In this part, Dr. Math explains

- tangents
- arcs and angles
- chords

Tangents

We can talk about a line or a segment being tangent to a single circle, but we can also have **common tangents**, which are tangent to two (or more) circles. In the picture below, line *IJ* is a common external tangent, and line *KL* is a common internal tangent.

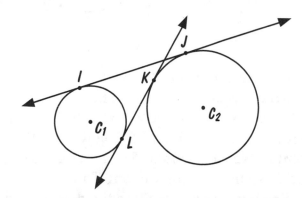

Tangents to Circles

Dear Dr. Math,

I want to try to prove that a line *l* is tangent to circle *C* if and only if *l* is perpendicular to *ZA*, where *Z* is the center of my circle and *A* is a point on circle *C*. My book gave me the hint to consider the Pythagorean theorem, but I am unsure of how to begin.

Yours truly,

Qian

Hi, Qian,

You didn't say this, but you need A to lie on l for your example to be true. You need to show that if l is perpendicular to ZA at A, then every point on l other than A is farther from Z than A is and therefore lies outside the circle. Let P be such a point. Then AZP is a right triangle, and you can use the Pythagorean theorem to show that ZP > AZ. Thus l and the circle meet at the single point A, which makes l a tangent.

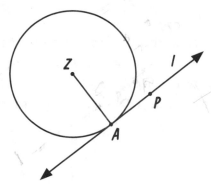

That takes care of the "if" part.

Now suppose that line l is not perpendicular to AZ, and construct a line perpendicular to l, through Z, meeting it at point Q. Let the point R be on l such that RQ = AQ and RA = 2 · AQ. Then show that point R lies on the circle. Thus l intersects the circle in two points, A and R, so line l is not tangent. That takes care of the "only if" part.

See if you can now fill in the details and the reasons.

—Dr. Math, The Math Forum

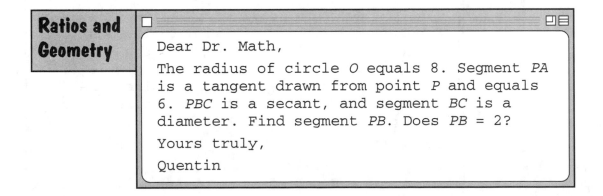

Ratios and Geometry

Dear Dr. Math,

The radius of circle O equals 8. Segment PA is a tangent drawn from point P and equals 6. PBC is a secant, and segment BC is a diameter. Find segment PB. Does PB = 2?

Yours truly,

Quentin

Hi, Quentin,

We can draw the situation you describe like this:

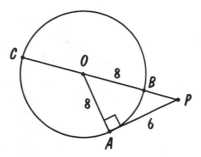

If we knew the length of PO, we could subtract BO and get PB. PA is tangent to the circle, so we know that there is a right angle at A. Since OAP is a right triangle, we can use the Pythagorean theorem to find that hypotenuse PO is 10. So yes, PB will be 2. Good work!

—Dr. Math, The Math Forum

The Distance between Points of Tangency

Dear Dr. Math,

Two circles, one of radius 5 and the other of radius 8, intersect at exactly one point, and the center of each circle lies outside the other circle. A line is externally tangent to both circles. Find the distance between the two points of tangency.

Yours truly,

Qian

Hi, Qian,

Let C_1 and C_2 be the centers of the two circles, where C_1 belongs to the circle with radius 5. Let T_1 and T_2 be the points of tangency of these circles with the common externally tangent line.

We know that $C_1T_1 = 5$ and $C_2T_2 = 8$ and that both are perpendicular to the common tangent T_1T_2. We also know that $C_1C_2 = 5 + 8 = 13$.

Now we have the following sketch:

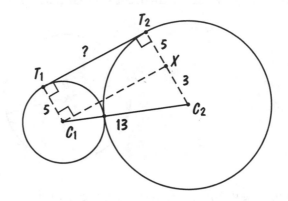

In this sketch, C_1X is parallel to T_1T_2 and thus perpendicular to T_2C_2. Now we can find C_1X and thus T_1T_2 by the Pythagorean theorem.

—*Dr. Math, The Math Forum*

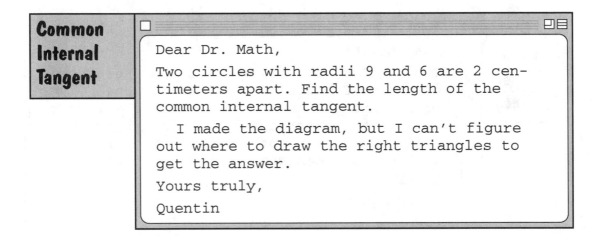

Common Internal Tangent

Dear Dr. Math,

Two circles with radii 9 and 6 are 2 centimeters apart. Find the length of the common internal tangent.

I made the diagram, but I can't figure out where to draw the right triangles to get the answer.

Yours truly,

Quentin

Hi, Quentin,

Let me describe the diagram I'm going to use. Points A and B are the centers of the two circles, and line segment AB connects them. Draw the common internal tangent and call point C its point of tangency with circle A, point D its point of tangency with circle B, and point E its intersection with segment AB.

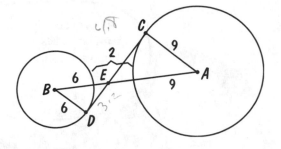

The first thing we'll see is that triangle *ACE* is similar to triangle *BDE*. Because tangent lines are perpendicular to the circle's radius at the point of tangency, ∠*ACE* is a right angle. Similarly, ∠*BDE* is a right angle. Right angles are congruent to each other. Since segments *AC* and *BD* are both perpendicular to *CD*, they are parallel to each other. So segment *AB* intersects the parallel segments *AC* and *BD*, making ∠*CAE* congruent to ∠*DBE* because they are alternate interior angles. Since triangles *ACE* and *BDE* have two pairs of congruent angles, they are similar triangles.

In similar triangles, corresponding parts are proportional to each other. Let's say that circle *A* is the bigger circle. Then *AC* = 9. The corresponding part of circle *B* is *BD*, which has length 6. Since *AC* is $\frac{3}{2}$ the size of *BD* and the two triangles are similar, any part of triangle *ACE* is $\frac{3}{2}$ larger than the corresponding part of triangle *BDE*.

We can use this information to find the length of segment *AE*. We know that *AB* = *AE* + *BE* = 6 + 9 + 2 = 17. Also, we know that *AE* is $\frac{3}{2}$ times the size of its corresponding part *BE* in the other triangle. So we have this system of two equations:

$$AE + BE = 17$$

$$AE = \frac{3}{2}BE$$

Can you find values of *AE* and *BE* that satisfy these equations? If you can, then you can use the Pythagorean theorem to find the lengths of segments *CE* and *DE*, and their sum is the length of *CD*, the common internal tangent.

—*Dr. Math, The Math Forum*

As we learn more about circles, it seems like we always need a diagram to show what we're thinking.

Yes, and geometry software and my computer sure help!

Intersecting Circles

Dear Dr. Math,

Two circles intersect at *A* and *B*. A common tangent touches the two circles at *S* and *T*. Show that the line *AB* bisects the common tangent *ST*.

I have tried various methods—for example, using the intercept theorem and circle properties—and I am still stumped. I would appreciate a solution.

Yours truly,

Qian

Hi, Qian,

One fact that we can use here is that the **power of a point** with regard to a circle is constant. This may sound confusing, but I think if you follow along with your own diagrams, you'll be fine.

What is the power of a point with respect to a circle? Let P be a point, and let a line through P intersect the circle at points L and M. Then the power of P with respect to the circle is $PL \cdot PM$. When P is inside the circle, the product is negative.

For this problem, we will consider P to be outside the circle. Why doesn't it matter what line through P intersects the circle? Let's look at a diagram:

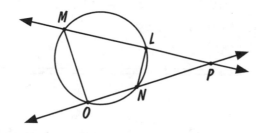

We can see that m$\angle PNL$ = 180 − m$\angle ONL$. We also know that m$\angle OML$ = 180 − m$\angle ONL$, since there is a theorem that says that opposite angles in a quadrilateral that is inscribed in a circle are supplementary. So we know that $\angle PNL \cong \angle OML$. We can show that $\angle PNL \cong \angle MON$ in the same way. So triangles PNL and PMO are similar. Thus $\frac{PN}{PL} = \frac{PM}{PO}$, and $PL \cdot PM = PN \cdot PO$. We can conclude that the power is constant.

When the line through P is tangent to a circle, say at point G, then, of course, the power of P with respect to the circle becomes $PG \cdot PG = PG^2$.

Now for your problem, let us consider a tangent common to two circles and the line connecting the intersection points of these circles:

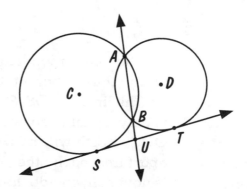

The power of U with respect to the circle with center C is
$US^2 = UB \cdot UA$.

The power of U with respect to the circle with center D is
$UT^2 = UB \cdot UA$.

So we have $US^2 = UT^2$, and hence $US = UT$, as required.

—Dr. Math, The Math Forum

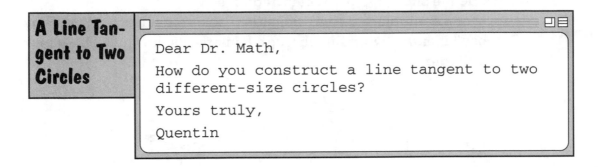

A Line Tangent to Two Circles

Dear Dr. Math,

How do you construct a line tangent to two different-size circles?

Yours truly,

Quentin

Hi, Quentin,

Let me use $\odot C_1$ and $\odot C_2$ for the two different-size circles with centers C_1 and C_2. Draw the line $l = C_1C_2$ and the perpendiculars to that line through C_1 and C_2.

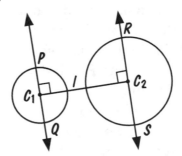

The line perpendicular to l at C_1 meets $\odot C_1$ at two points, P and Q, and the line perpendicular to l at C_2 meets $\odot C_2$ at points R and S.

The lines PR, QS, PS, and QR intersect l at two points: A and B. It is only useful to consider these points if they are outside $\odot C_1$ and $\odot C_2$, as both will be when the two circles do not intersect and are apart from each other; one of them will be outside when one circle is not totally inside the other one.

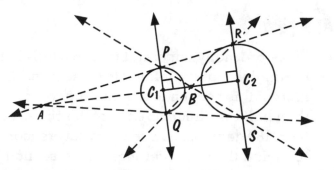

A and B are the starting points for possible tangents to both circles. If a tangent starts from, for instance, A, then the reflection of that tangent through *l* is, of course, a tangent, too, and thus two (or zero) tangents start from one point.

Now you can construct the tangents from, for instance, A to $\odot C_1$ in the following way:

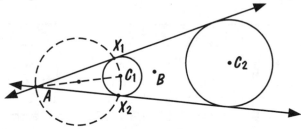

Draw the circle having AC_1 as the diameter and find the intersection points of this circle with C_1, say X_1 and X_2. The lines AX_1 and AX_2 are the two tangents we look for.

When two circles do not intersect and neither circle is inside the other, you will find a total of four common tangents to those circles.

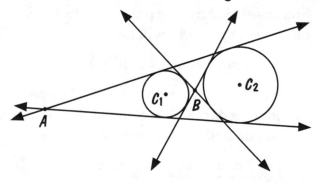

—Dr. Math, The Math Forum

Arcs and Angles

There are many important relationships between arcs of circles and the angles that are related to those arcs. The arc shown in the beginning of this section is a *minor* arc, which means that it covers less than half the circumference of the circle. Its degree measure is less than 180 degrees. (A major arc covers more than half the circumference, and a semicircle covers exactly half.) The degree measure of an arc is equal to the angle measure of the central angle that **subtends** that arc. In the figure, arc *AB* has a measure of 67 degrees, while arc *CD* has a measure of 214 degrees.

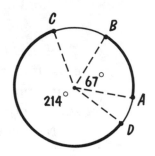

Arc Formulas

Dear Dr. Math,

I am trying to determine the angle of an arc from the radius and arc length. The radius is 630 and the arc length is 66.82.

How can I remember the formula?

Yours truly,

Qian

Hi, Qian,

Suppose you have a circle with radius 660 centimeters. The circumference of the circle will be

$$\text{circumference} = 2 \cdot 660 \cdot \pi$$

Right? That corresponds to 360 degrees, since it goes all the way around the circle. Since you have just a part of that arc length, you can set up and solve a proportion:

$$\frac{? \text{ degrees}}{360 \text{ degrees}} = \frac{66.82 \text{ cm}}{(2 \cdot 660 \cdot \pi) \text{ cm}}$$

Consider some test cases to see why this works. If your arc is the same as the circumference, you should end up with 360 degrees, and you do. If your arc is half the circumference, you should end up with 180 degrees, and you do.

Basically, the ratio of the arc length to the circumference is the same as the ratio of the angle to the whole 360 degrees of the circle. Does that make sense?

—Dr. Math, The Math Forum

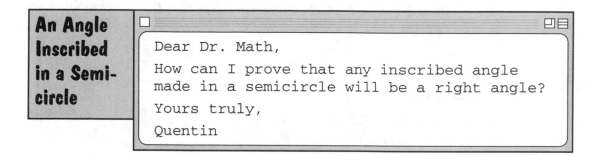

An Angle Inscribed in a Semicircle

Dear Dr. Math,

How can I prove that any inscribed angle made in a semicircle will be a right angle?

Yours truly,

Quentin

Hi, Quentin,

Let's consider a circle with its center at point C. Let's say that line segment PQ is a diameter of this circle and that point R is some other point on the circle. Then arc PRQ is a semicircle, and we want to prove that ∠PRQ is a right angle.

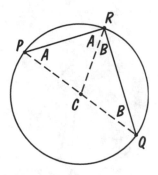

Looking at this diagram, we don't know much besides the fact that P, Q, and R are all points on a circle with its center at C. And since all points on a circle are equally distant from the center, we can conclude that segments PC, QC, and RC are all congruent.

Now let's try to relate this to some of the angles in the diagram. If *PC* and *RC* are congruent, *PCR* is an isosceles triangle, and the base angles *CPR* and *CRP* are congruent. For future reference, I'm going to call the measure of these congruent angles A. Similarly, since *RC* and *QC* are congruent, *QCR* is an isosceles triangle, and the base angles *CQR* and *CRQ* are congruent. Let's call the measure of these congruent angles B.

Since ∠*PRQ* is the sum of angles *CRP* and *CRQ*, what we're really trying to prove is that A + B is 90 degrees. The sum of the three angles in any triangle is 180 degrees. Applying this to isosceles triangle *PCR*, we get

$$2A + \angle PCR = 180$$

and applying it to isosceles triangle QCR, we get

$$2B + \angle QCR = 180$$

and adding these two equations together, we get

$$2A + 2B + \angle PCR + \angle QCR = 360$$

But PQ is a straight line segment and it's the diameter of the circle, so C lies on it, and PCR and QCR are supplementary angles. So the sum of their measures is 180 degrees, and we now have

$$2A + 2B + 180 = 360$$
$$2A + 2B = 180$$
$$A + B = 90$$

which is what we want to prove. $\angle PRQ$, which measures $A + B$, has 90 degrees. It is a right angle.

—Dr. Math, The Math Forum

The Inscribed Angle Theorem

Dear Dr. Math,

I'm trying to find a proof for the theorem stating that any angle inscribed on the same arc as a central angle is one-half that central angle, where the vertex of the angle is on the circle's circumference.

Yours truly,

Qian

Hi, Qian,

Consider a circle centered at C. Let DA be a diameter of this circle and let B be another point on the circle. You want to show that the angle on arc AB from C is double the angle on arc AB from D. Here is a figure for your reference:

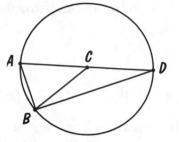

We see that $\angle ACB + \angle BCD = 180$ degrees, $\angle BCD + \angle DBC + \angle CDB = 180$ degrees, and triangle BDC is isosceles, so we can conclude that $\angle ACB = 2 \cdot \angle CDB = 2 \cdot \angle ADB$.

This proves your theorem for angles with one leg passing through the center of the circle. Other cases can be proved by adding a diameter to the figure. You can apply the simpler form twice in that new situation. Either adding or subtracting these two gives the proof. As an example, consider the situation in the following figure:

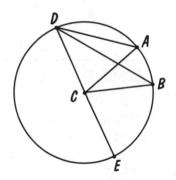

For the theorem we should have to prove that $\angle BCA = 2 \cdot \angle BDA$. In this figure, the simpler form shows us that

$$\angle ECB = 2 \cdot \angle EDB$$

$$\angle ECA = 2 \cdot \angle EDA$$

But then also

$$\angle BCA = \angle ECA - \angle ECB$$

$$= 2 \cdot (\angle EDA - \angle EDB)$$

$$= 2 \cdot \angle BDA$$

—*Dr. Math, The Math Forum*

Tangents and Arcs

Dear Dr. Math,

There are two tangent segments from a point to a circle. Say that the angle formed by the two tangents is 80 degrees. How would you go about proving that the arc closest to the angle formed by the two tangents and that angle are supplementary, so therefore the arc is 100?

Yours truly,

Quentin

Hi, Quentin,

Draw three lines. First, draw the line that goes through the center of the circle and the given point. This line bisects the angle formed by the two tangents. (Why?) Then draw two radii from the center of the circle to each point of tangency on the circle. Each radius is perpendicular to the tangent line it touches. (Again, why?)

So we have two congruent right triangles. Since the sum of the angles of each triangle is 180 and the triangle is right, it follows that half the angle of the intercepted arc is complementary to half the angle formed by the tangent lines. Multiplying by 2 gives the desired relationship.

Here is a figure for your reference:

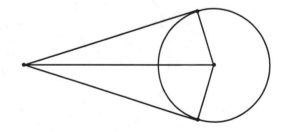

—Dr. Math, The Math Forum

Chords

Knowing how chords of circles are related to one another and to the radii of those circles can help you calculate many different relationships, even when you think you don't have enough information.

Finding the Center of a Circle

Dear Dr. Math,

How do you find the center of a circle if you don't know anything about it except its physical shape?

Yours truly,

Qian

Hi, Qian,

If you have a straightedge (unmarked ruler) and a compass, it is easy to locate the center of a circle. Draw any line *l* through the circle so that it intersects the circle at *A* and *B*. Then with the compass, find the perpendicular bisector of *AB*, which will intersect the circle at *C* and *D*. Clearly, *CD* is a diameter, so if you bisect *CD* at point *O*, *O* is the center of the circle.

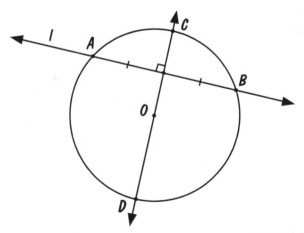

—*Dr. Math, The Math Forum*

Hi, Dr. Math,

I thought you'd like to hear a real-world application of your solution. [See "Finding the Center of a Circle" on page 146.]

I was trying to move a doorknob from an old door to a new one. When a doorknob is purchased new, it comes with a paper template that the builder can fold over the edge of the door. An X on the template marks the center of the big hole to be drilled. But with an old doorknob, I had to create my own template from the old door.

First, I folded a blank paper over the edge of the old door and traced the outlines of the old hole. This gave me the circle to be drilled but not the center. Then I used your method to mark the center of the circle. Then I folded the new template over the edge of the new door and drilled where I had marked. It worked perfectly! Thanks for your solution!

Qian

Chords of Circles: The Distance from the Center

Dear Dr. Math,

There is a circle with radius 10 and a chord *XY* that is 8 centimeters long. How far is the chord from *O*, the center of the circle?

I cannot figure this out. My book has congruent chords and the distance to one chord, so it's in the diagram and all you do is substitute. But in this case, I do not know how to start.

Yours truly,

Quentin

Hi, Quentin,

Draw the circle and chord *AB*. Now draw lines from the center *O* of the circle to the ends of the chord, *A* and *B*. Finally, draw a line from the center of the circle to the midpoint of the chord, *C*.

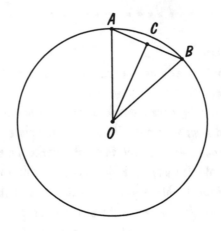

Now let's look at the diagram. Can you see that *OC* is the perpendicular bisector of *AB*? That gives you a right triangle *OCA*. You know the lengths of *OA* and *AC*. The Pythagorean theorem can help you find *OC*.

—*Dr. Math, The Math Forum*

Dear Dr. Math,

In any circle:

1. A radius that is perpendicular to a chord also bisects the chord. I tried adding in triangles, but I don't know how to prove it.

2. A radius that bisects the chord is perpendicular to the chord. I don't know how to prove that, either.

3. Chords that are equidistant from the center of the circle are congruent. Still can't prove it.

It would really be great if you could help me. Thanks.

Yours truly,

Qian

Hi, Qian,

Those are good theorems to know! Let me get you started on each of them. For the first two cases, draw a diagram like the one below:

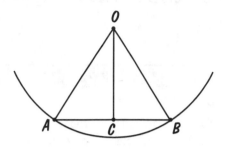

O is the center of the circle; *AB* is the chord.

OA = *OB* because they are radii of the circle.

1. *OC* is perpendicular to *AB*. Use the Pythagorean theorem in triangles *OCA* and *OCB*.

2. *OC* bisects *AB*. *CA* = *CB*. Use side-side-side (SSS) to conclude that triangles *OCA* and *OCB* are congruent. Then ∠*ACO* = ∠*BCO*. Because *AB* is a straight line, you know that ∠*ACO* + ∠*BCO* = 180 degrees, so ∠*ACO* and ∠*BCO* are both right angles, which means that the radius is perpendicular to the chord.

3. For this part, use a diagram like this:

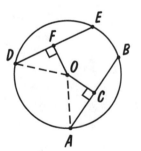

OC is congruent to *OF*, and we want to prove that *AB* is congruent to *DE*. *OA* and *OD* are radii, so they're congruent. ∠*OCA* and ∠*OFD* are right angles by definition (because that's how you measure distance). We've got two sides of a right triangle corresponding to two sides of another right triangle; therefore, triangles *OCA* and *OFD* are congruent. (Think of the Pythagorean theorem.) Since they're corresponding parts, *AC* and *DF* are congruent. By your proof above, *OC* bisects *AB*, and *OF* bisects *DE*. So *AB* is congruent to *DE*.

—Dr. Math, The Math Forum

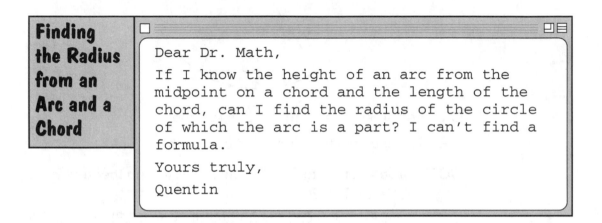

Finding the Radius from an Arc and a Chord

Dear Dr. Math,

If I know the height of an arc from the midpoint on a chord and the length of the chord, can I find the radius of the circle of which the arc is a part? I can't find a formula.

Yours truly,

Quentin

Hi, Quentin,

We can work out the formula this way. You know the length of the chord, which we'll call c, and the height of the arc above the known chord, which we'll call h. We now know that the rest of the radius that contains h has a length of r − h.

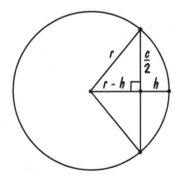

Since a radius through the midpoint of a chord is perpendicular to the chord, we have a right triangle, and the Pythagorean theorm gives

$$r^2 = (r - h)^2 + \left(\frac{c}{2}\right)^2$$

$$r^2 = r^2 - 2rh + h^2 + \frac{c^2}{4}$$

$$2rh = h^2 + \frac{c^2}{4}$$

$$r = \frac{h^2 + \dfrac{c^2}{4}}{2h} = \frac{4h^2 + c^2}{8h}$$

—Dr. Math, The Math Forum

Intersecting Chords

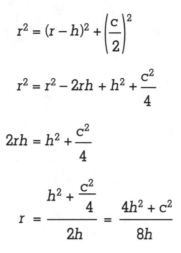

Dear Dr. Math,

There are two chords inscribed in a circle, *AB* and *CD*. They intersect at point *E*. Prove that *AE · EB = CE · ED*.

First, I drew chords *AD* and *CB* to create two triangles. The vertical angles *AED* and *CEB* are congruent and so are angles *AEC* and *DEB*. But I am lost from there. I know I should prove that the two triangles are similar triangles, but I'm still not entirely certain how much that will aid me in this proof.

Is it possible the proof was phrased wrong and it means that *AE · EB* is proportional to *CE · ED*?

Yours truly,

Qian

Hi, Qian,

Consider the following figure:

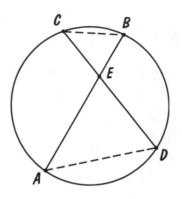

Indeed, ∠AED and ∠BEC are congruent vertical angles. Also, ∠DAB and ∠DCB are congruent, because they are inscribed angles on the same arc. In a similar fashion, ∠CDA and ∠CBA are congruent.

This shows us that triangles BCE and DAE are similar (note that B corresponds to D and C to A). From that,

$$\frac{BE}{CE} = \frac{ED}{EA}$$

$$BE \cdot EA = CE \cdot ED$$

—*Dr. Math, The Math Forum*

esources on the Web

Learn more about circles at these Math Forum sites:

Geometry Problem of the Week: Arc to Area

mathforum.org/geopow/solutions/solution.ehtml?puzzle=219

Given an arc with a measure of 40 degrees whose endpoints are at (1,5) and (5,3), find the area of the circle that contains the arc.

Geometry Problem of the Week: Building a Vaulted Ceiling

mathforum.org/geopow/solutions/solution.ehtml?puzzle=96

An eyebrow window is a 15-inch-deep slice off an 8.5-foot circle. How wide will the base of the window be?

Geometry Problem of the Week: Circles and Tangents

mathforum.org/geopow/solutions/solution.ehtml?puzzle=71

AOD is a diameter of circle *O*. *B* is any point on the circle. A tangent is drawn to the circle at *B*. A line is drawn parallel to *AB* from the center *O*, meeting the tangent at *P*. Prove that *PD* is tangent to the circle.

Geometry Problem of the Week: Circumnavigating Circles

mathforum.org/geopow/solutions/solution.ehtml?puzzle=217

The radii of two wheels are 10 vershoks and 5 vershoks, and their centers are 30 vershoks apart. A belt goes around both of the wheels, crisscrossing between the two centers to form two internal tangents. What's the length of the belt?

Geometry Problem of the Week: Tangents and a Triangle

mathforum.org/geopow/archive/031497.geopow.html

AB and *CB* are tangents to a circle, with *A* and *C* on the circle and *B* at their intersection. *D* is a point on the minor arc *AC*, and a tangent is drawn at *D* that intersects *AB* at *E* and *CB* at *F*. What is the perimeter of *EFB*?

Geometry Problem of the Week: What Do We Know about Tangents?

mathforum.org/geopow/solutions/solution.ehtml?puzzle=32

Given two externally tangent congruent circles, construct a segment from the center of one circle tangent to the other circle. If the length of this segment is 10, what's the radius of the circles?

Glossary......................................

adjacent angles   Angles sharing a vertex and one side.

alternate exterior angles   In a figure involving parallel lines crossed by a transversal, angles on alternate sides of the transversal—both *outside* the parallel lines.

alternate interior angles   In a figure involving parallel lines crossed by a transversal, angles on alternate sides of the transversal—both *inside* the parallel lines.

altitude   In a triangle, a line segment from a vertex to the opposite side or the line that contains the opposite side perpendicular to that line. Its length is the height of the triangle.

angle bisector   The locus of points that have equal distances to the sides of the angle, dividing the angle into two angles of equal measure.

arc   A continuous portion of a circle bounded by two points.

area   The portion of a plane covered by a closed figure.

axiom   See **postulate**.

base   A side or face considered as the bottom part, or foundation, of a geometric figure. In an isosceles triangle, the side that is not a leg, or is not equal in length to another side; in a quadrilateral, the side you consider as the flat-on-the-ground side for the purpose of measurement; in three dimensions, any side of a figure designated as such, often one that is flat on the ground from the viewer's perspective.

central angle   An angle whose vertex is the center of a circle.

centroid   The intersection of the medians of a triangle.

chord   A segment connecting any two points on a circle.

circumcenter   The intersection of the perpendicular bisectors of the sides of a triangle.

circumscribed circle   A circle drawn around a figure so that the figure's vertices lie on the circle.

collinear   Lying on the same line.

common tangent   A line tangent to two or more circles.

concave polygon   A polygon in which at least one interior angle measures greater than 180 degrees.

conclusion   The "then" part of an "if-then" conditional statement.

conditional statement   A logic sentence with a condition in it; often phrased as "If . . . then . . . ."

congruent   Having the same dimensions. If you put congruent shapes on transparent paper and hold them up on top of each other, you can't tell them apart.

contrapositive   The negation of both the hypothesis and the conclusion in a conditional statement as well as the reversal of the two parts. The contrapositive of "If A, then B" is "If not B, then not A."

converse   The reversal of the hypothesis and the conclusion in a conditional statement. The converse of "If A, then B" is "If B, then A."

convex polygon   A polygon whose interior angles all measure less than 180 degrees.

corresponding angles   In a figure involving parallel lines crossed by a transversal, angles in corresponding positions relative to the transversal on different parallel lines.

diameter   A chord passing through the center of a circle; twice the radius.

equilateral triangle   A regular triangle; a triangle having equal sides and equal angles.

Euler line   The line passing through the orthocenter, circumcenter, and centroid of a triangle.

hypotenuse   The side opposite the right angle in a right triangle.

hypothesis   The "if" part of an "if-then" conditional statement. Also called the "premise."

incenter   The intersection of the angle bisectors of a triangle.

inscribed angle   An angle whose vertex is on a circle, and whose rays contain chords of the circle.

inverse   The negation of both the hypothesis and the conclusion in a conditional statement. The inverse of "If A, then B" is "If not A, then not B."

isosceles triangle   A triangle with at least two equal legs.

kite   A quadrilateral with two pairs of adjacent sides with equal lengths. (The other common definition, one we don't use in this book, says that the two pairs must have different lengths, meaning a rhombus and a square are not special cases of a kite.)

legs   The sides of an isosceles triangle that have equal length; or the sides of a right triangle that are adjacent to the right angle.

linear pair of angles   Adjacent angles whose nonshared sides lie on one line and whose angle measures sum to 180.

median   A line segment from a vertex of a triangle to the midpoint of the opposite side.

orthocenter   The intersection of a triangle's altitudes.

parallelogram   A quadrilateral with exactly two pairs of parallel sides.

perimeter   The distance around the edges of a figure, especially a polygon.

perpendicular bisector   A line that divides a segment in half and is at right angles to the segment.

polygon   A two-dimensional closed figure made up of straight line segments.

postulate   A statement accepted as true without needing proof.

power of a point   Let P be a point, and let a line through P intersect the circle at points L and M. Then the power of P with respect to the circle is $PL \cdot PM$. When P is inside the circle, the product is negative.

premise   See **hypothesis**.

Pythagorean theorem   In a right triangle, the sum of the squares of the lengths of the legs is equal to the square of the length of the hypotenuse.

radius   A segment connecting the center of a circle with a point on the circle; or the length of such a segment.

rectangle   A quadrilateral in which all angles have the same measure (90 degrees).

reflexive   The property that says an object is congruent to itself.

rhombus   A quadrilateral in which all sides have the same length.

scale factor   The ratio by which a copy of a figure is larger or smaller than its original image.

scalene quadrilateral   A quadrilateral with unequal and nonparallel sides.

secant   A line or a segment intersecting a circle at two points.

similar   Two figures are similar if their corresponding angles are equal and their corresponding line segments are in proportion.

square   A quadrilateral in which all sides have the same length and all angles are right angles.

subtend   To be opposite from and extend to the ends of; the central angle whose sides mark the endpoints of an arc subtends that arc.

symmetric   The property that says if object A is congruent to object B, then object B is congruent to object A.

tangent   A line or segment intersecting a circle at exactly one point perpendicular to the circle's radius at that point.

transitive   The property that says if object A is congruent to object B and object B is congruent to object C, then object A is congruent to object C.

trapezoid   A quadrilateral that has at least one pair of parallel sides. (According to the other definition commonly in use, one we don't use in this book, a trapezoid is a quadrilateral with exactly one pair of parallel sides.)

vertical angles   The angles on opposite sides of the vertex formed when two lines cross.

Index..

finding radius from arcs and, 150–151

   intersecting, 151–152

   theorems involving, 148–150

circles

   arcs and angles, 140–145

   area of, 114

   center of, 146–147

   chords, 130, 146–152

   circumscribed, 160

   common external tangents, 131,
     133–134

   common internal tangents, 131,
     134–136

   distance between points of tan-
     gency, 133–134

   intersecting, 136–138

   line tangent to two, constructing,
     138–139

   parts of, 130

   ratios and, 132–133

   resources on the Web, 152–153

   tangents to, 50, 131–132

circumcenter of triangles, 60

circumscribed circles, 60

collinear points, 9–10

common tangents to circles, 131,
   133–136

concave polygons, 93, 94–96, 98

conclusions, 29

conditional statements and logic,
   31–33

congruence

  in triangles, 66–75, 80–85

congruent angles, 7

contrapositive, 30

  converse, definition of, 29, 30

convex quadrilaterals, 92, 94

coordinate geometry, 20–25

corresponding angles, 7

CPCTC (corresponding parts of congruent triangles are congruent),
   80–81

D

degrees in triangles, 16–17

diameter, 130

direct proofs, 49

distance between points of tangency,
   133–134

distance formula, 20, 22–25, 105–106

E

elliptical geometry, 18–19

equation of a line, 22

equilateral triangles, properties of, 62,
   64–66

Euclidean geometry

  fifth postulate of, 14–15

  parallel postulate and, 4, 17

Euler line of triangle, 60

exterior angles of polygons, 94–96

F

formulas, memorizing, 2, 140–141

G

Geometer's Sketchpad, 72

geometry

  coordinate, 20–25

  definition of, 27

  elliptical, 18

  Euclidean, 4, 14–15, 17

  hyperbolic, 18, 19

  non-Euclidean, 16–19

  spherical, 18

  tips for success with, 1–2

  uses of, 27–28

Global Positioning System (GPS)
   devices, 27

H

height

  of buildings, using shadows to
   measure, 77–78

of parallelograms, 112–113
of trapezoid, 106–108
HL (hypotenuse-leg) shortcut, 74, 77
hyperbolic geometry, 18, 19
hypotenuse, 11
hypotenuse-leg (HL) shortcut, 74, 77
hypothesis, 29

I

incenter of triangles, 61
indirect proofs, 49–54
inscribed angles, 130
inscribed angle theorem, 143–144
interior angles of polygons, 91–94,
    97–98
intersecting chords, 151–152
intersecting circles, 136–138
inverse, 30
irregular polygons, area of, 125–127
isosceles triangles
    angles of, 62–64
    proofs and, 58–59
    properties of, 62

K

kites, 100

L

legs of triangles, 11, 62
linear pairs of angles, 6
lines
    definition of, 3–4
    in hyperbolic geometry, 19
    intersecting at one point, 9
    intersection in one plane, 8–10,
        17–19
    perpendicular, 5, 10–11, 104
    resources on the Web, 25–26
    in spherical geometry, 18
    See also parallel lines
line segments, midpoints of, 21

logic
    conditional statements and, 31–33
    contrapositive, finding, 30–31
    converse, finding, 30–31
    determining truth of statement and
        converse, 28–29
    inverse, finding, 30–31
    proofs and, 34–36
    resources on the Web, 54
    symbols p and q in statements of, 31

M

major arcs, 140
measuring height of buildings using
    shadows, 77–78
medians of triangles, 53–54, 58–59
memorizing formulas, 2, 140–141
midpoints of line segments, 21
minor arcs, 140

N

naming angles, 6
non-Euclidean geometry, 16–19

O

orthocenter of triangles, 60

P

paragraph proofs, 34
parallel lines
    definition of, 5
    intersection of, 10
    in non-Euclidean geometries, 17–18
    proving, 12–13, 46–49
    theorem, 51–54
parallelograms
    angle measures in, 101
    area of, 116, 121–123
    description of, 99
    perimeter of, 102–103, 111–113
    proving perpendicular diagonals,
        103–105